Helping At-Risk Students

Helping At-Risk Students

A Group Counseling Approach for Grades 6–9

Jill Waterman

Elizabeth Walker

The Guilford Press
New York London

© 2001 The Guilford Press
A Division of Guilford Publications, Inc.
72 Spring Street, New York, NY 10012
www.guilford.com

Printed in the United States of America

This book is printed on acid-free paper.

Last digit is print number: 9 8 7 6 5 4 3 2 1

Library of Congress Cataloging-in-Publication Data is available from the Publisher.

ISBN 1-57230-571-1

To my sons, Justy and Aaron, who experienced the 6th through 10th grades during the continuing evolution of the counseling program, frequently giving me insights, inspiring me, setting me straight, and often humbling me. They are terrific!

    —J. W.

To my family, whose love and support have made me who I am. And to my husband, Ryan, whose goodness and wisdom are a constant reminder of the person I would like to be.

    —E. W.

To the many wonderful young people who have participated in our groups. Their energy, enthusiasm, and love of life, as well as their pain, have touched our minds and our hearts in so many ways.

    —J. W. and E. W.

About the Authors

Jill Waterman, PhD, is an adjunct professor of psychology at the University of California, Los Angeles, and coordinator of the UCLA Psychology Clinic, the training clinic for UCLA's top-ranked PhD program in clinical psychology. In addition to numerous articles on aspects of child trauma, she is the coauthor of *Sexual Abuse of Young Children: Evaluation and Treatment* and *Behind the Playground Walls: Sexual Abuse in Preschools.* Her research focuses on various aspects of child trauma and on developing and evaluating interventions aimed at helping our most vulnerable children. Dr. Waterman is also a practicing psychotherapist in the Los Angeles area and has 16-year-old twin sons.

Elizabeth Walker, PhD, received her doctorate in clinical psychology from UCLA in 2000. As a graduate student, she spent several years working with adolescents in inner-city schools, and she completed her predoctoral internship at the University of California, San Diego's Psychology Internship Consortium in 2000. Dr. Walker's research interests include understanding the role of religion and spirituality in the lives of young people, as well as developing and implementing interventions for at-risk youth. She currently lives in the San Diego area with her husband.

Preface

Aimed at helping our most vulnerable young adolescents, this book attempts to provide tools and techniques for practitioners working with youth at risk for academic, behavioral, and emotional difficulties that result from such factors as difficult family situations, learning problems, or socioeconomic disadvantage. The curriculum, which we call SPARK because it is intended to spark greater student achievement, social-emotional growth, and nonviolent responding, combines a group process model aimed at developing interpersonal skills and a psychoeducational model focused on building competence by development of specific skills needed by all youth, and particularly needed by at-risk youth. The goals are to provide a trusting, supportive environment that facilitates discussion and disclosure regarding, for example, educational goals, aggression and violence, ethnic identity and discrimination, and interpersonal relationships; and to teach specific skills such as anger management, interpersonal conflict resolution, effective study skills, communication tools, and peer pressure resistance.

The SPARK curriculum has seven modules, each with several sessions. Each of the modules addresses issues salient for at-risk youth (Trust Building and Communication Skills; Anger Management and Problem-Solving Skills; Ethnic Identity and Anti-Prejudice; Educational Aspirations; Peer Pressure and Gangs; Exposure to Violence and Posttraumatic Stress Reactions; and Family Relationships). The modules can be ex-panded to fit the needs of a particular school or group. For example, if a group contains several very aggressive students, the Anger Management and Problem-Solving module can be extended as needed. Similarly, modules that do not seem relevant for a particular school or group can be dropped. Designed to help students who may be turned off by school, SPARK groups are activity-based, engaging, and interactive. The curriculum can be helpful for students who are already experiencing problems and can be used as a tool to prevent problems from developing.

The program can be utilized in a variety of settings. We have focused primarily on the school setting in accordance with the trend for mental health and social services for children to be increasingly school-based. The school provides an important location for such programs as SPARK, which are aimed at high-risk students who often would not otherwise have access to such prevention and intervention services, due to lack of community resources or family difficulties. The curriculum was developed in a small-group setting; however, most of the activities in the curriculum can easily be adapted for use with whole classrooms. The activities come with discussion questions and major points that can easily be used by classroom teachers. Within the school setting, the curriculum can be implemented successfully by a wide range of school-based practitioners, including school psychologists, guidance counselors, school social workers, school nurses, other administrative school personnel, and interested teachers. In addition, graduate students in education, social work, and psychology can implement the curriculum in collaboration with school personnel.

In addition to school professionals, the curriculum has been used successfully by social workers, psychologists, and other allied health personnel in mental health settings, including outpatient groups and day treatment settings for adolescents. Some of the activities require a small- or large-group setting, but some can be utilized in individual counseling within both school and clinic settings. The program can also be used by university-based trainers working with students preparing for careers in education, psychology, and social work.

SPARK evolved over a period of years, but began with a few groups meeting after school in housing projects in Los Angeles. In these settings we saw very vividly some of the issues faced daily by at-risk youth. The playgrounds and sandboxes were strewn with broken glass and even spent bullet casings, and gang members hung out at the side of the buildings and occasionally menaced passersby. Once an adult resident burst into the room where our group was being held and asked if he could stay because he was being chased by a man with a gun who was trying to kill him. Many of the children often heard gunfire when home, had parents dealing with drug addiction or in jail, and had heavy responsibilities such as caring for younger children. Through such experiences, we realized the level of fear and uncertainty, the chronic exposure to violence, and the lack of supportive resources that confronted these young adolescents every day of their lives. We discovered that any curriculum that would eventually evolve would have to address issues of anger management, exposure to violence, and family relationships.

When presented with the opportunity to move the program to selected public schools, we were glad to proceed, because we felt we could reach a larger group of students. We developed our first informal curriculum in 1992, and have spent the last $7\frac{1}{2}$ years refining the activities and the format, based on work and field testing with over 375 adolescents in the sixth through the ninth grades. Activities were revised both to increase the interest level to students and to teach each skill as effectively as possible. We found that the groups were more successful when we gave the participants handouts and when we reinforced the major points made at the end of each session. In addition, we generated information about how to select members and start groups, counseling techniques useful in working with children in this stage of development, and ideas for handling possible trouble spots or dilemmas. After many refinements over several years, we decided that it was time to stop revising and start disseminating.

Through working in challenging settings, we have found implementation of the program to be very rewarding. Each student who learns nonviolent ways of responding to aggression and actually uses these new skills, who is able to resist peer pressure to join a gang or have sex, who develops greater understanding and tolerance for those who are ethnically different, who is able to support another group member, friend, or classmate in crisis, or who comes to terms with a past traumatic violent event is an affirmation of the importance of reaching out to these young and very vulnerable students. We envision SPARK being utilized in schools across the country to help today's troubled and vulnerable youth cope with the stresses they face in their families and communities. We hope that you will find utilization of the curriculum and the book to be a powerful and rewarding experience as you work to touch and positively impact the lives of at-risk youth.

Acknowledgments

This project has been a collaborative one, involving many people during the 8 years over which it has developed. The program originally began in the housing projects of Los Angeles, when we were working with John Pusey of the 4-H Urban Youth program of Cooperative Extension of the University of California. The project moved into the schools and became part of CUES (Community–University Enrichment in the Schools), a multifaceted project involving the UCLA Department of Psychology and several schools in the Los Angeles Unified School District 2 years later. CUES was funded for 3 years by the U.S. Department of Education, National Institute of Education (DOED P252A20055-94). The overall CUES project was headed by Seymour Feshbach, PhD, with Jennifer Abe-Kim, PhD, and then Curtiss Rooks serving very effectively as project directors. When the funding ended in 1994, only the group counseling project survived; it has continued on a shoestring budget with help from the Los Angeles Unified School District and the volunteer work of many UCLA students and school staff.

We give our heartfelt thanks to the many students in the UCLA PhD program in clinical psychology who served as project coordinators for the CUES group-counseling component, which formed the basis for the SPARK program: Jacqueline Raia, PhD, Sukey Egger, PhD, David Watt, PhD, Rose Corona, PhD, Liza Suarez, MA, and Anastasia Kim, MA. In addition to serving as project coordinators, all the above team members also co-led multiple counseling groups. Also co-leading multiple groups over several years were Jennifer Wood, PhD, Kimberly King, PhD, Nangel Lindberg, PhD, Silvia Gutierrez, MA, Tene Lewis, MA, and Antonio Polo, MA. Sukey Egger and David Watt were instrumental in organizing and expanding the manual content to make it easier for new leaders to lead groups. In addition to her other valuable roles, Liza Suarez translated the curriculum materials, handouts, and supporting materials into Spanish, helped format all the appendices, and gave useful suggestions in statistical analyses of the data. These graduate students who comprise our staff are nothing short of fantastic, working long hours without pay for the joy of helping at-risk minority students. Our undergraduate students carry out postgroup interviews and code and enter data. They too are dedicated and care very much for the middle-school and high-school students who participated in the project. In fact, as a result of their experiences, several of the undergraduates decided to go into school counseling or administration. Pam Marks, Administrative Officer for the clinical psychology program, was helpful in many small ways that meant so much in crisis situations. Jill Waterman's son Justy Burdick was invaluable in helping with manuscript preparation and formatting the appendices.

In the schools, we were fortunate to work with dedicated principals, administrative staff, and counselors who provided space for the groups to meet, photocopying, and other administrative help, and who made and coordinated referrals to the groups. Above all, our school liaisons believed that all at-risk students, regardless of their backgrounds and hardships, could succeed if given needed assistance.

Last and most importantly, we thank the approximately 400 students who have par-ticipated in groups over the last 7 years. They are inspiring, lovable, energetic, fun, and completely awesome, and we hope their futures will be brighter as a result of their participation.

Contents

Helping At-Risk Students

CHAPTER ONE

Guidelines for Setting Up and Leading Groups

The structured psychoeducational group counseling approach for at-risk youth to be presented was developed at UCLA with Los Angeles area schools over a period of six years. Intended to address issues salient to middle-school and high-school students who are struggling with academic, behavioral, and emotional difficulties, the curriculum is a 15-week program meant to span a school semester. This chapter covers the goals of the program, how to get groups started, the structure of the groups, group counseling techniques, and dilemmas for group leaders. In Chapter Two, the curriculum is presented, with detailed instructions on how to conduct each session. Chapter Three gives information on group participants and on the effectiveness of the program, followed by References and Appendixes with curriculum materials available for reproduction and use. Most activities can be adapted easily for use in the classroom. We have called the program SPARK because it is meant to spark increases in student achievement, social-emotional growth, and nonviolent responding. Having a name helps to uniquely identify the program within the school and allows students to feel connected to the program. Therefore, we have referred to the program as SPARK throughout the book; however, if another name seems more appropriate in a particular school or setting, it can be substituted.

Goals of the SPARK Program

The goals of the program are as follows:

1. To provide a trusting, supportive group environment that facilitates discussion and disclosure with peers.
2. To build competence by teaching specific skills, such as anger management, empathic responding, interpersonal problem resolution, resisting peer pressure, and communication skills.
3. To provide activities and discussion to facilitate exploration of issues of concern to youth, including educational goals, aggression and violence, ethnic identity, prejudice and discrimination, family relationships, and dating relationships.

Getting Started

Selecting Group Members

SPARK groups are intended for preadolescents and adolescents who are experiencing or are at risk for a variety of academic, behavioral, and emotional problems. Examples of common referral problems are: "Johnny's grades have dropped from B's to D's and F's in the last year"; "Isobel saw her brother get shot in a drive-by shooting last month and has been in a fog ever since";

"Michael seems angry all the time and gets into fights when waiting for the bus after school"; "Fernando cries at the drop of a hat and says he doesn't care if he lives or dies." Other common reasons for student referrals include depression, anxiety, angry outbursts, exposure to family or community violence, family conflict, and loss of a family member. The groups seem to be most successful when there is a balance between members who are more outgoing and those who are quieter. If all members are very quiet, it is difficult to develop lively discussions, while if most members need to be the center of attention, it is difficult to accomplish the tasks for each session.

When recruiting group members, it is important to consider characteristics of potential members that are likely to help rather than hinder the group process. Extremely disruptive youth should be excluded because they prevent other members from benefiting from the group; these students' needs may best be met through individual counseling. It is best to exclude children who are frequently absent, since such students generally miss many sessions and retard development of group cohesion. However, we occasionally have had participants who are chronically truant but come to school only to attend the counseling groups.

If there are major long-standing interpersonal conflicts between two potential group members (i.e., gang vendetta), it is best to place them in separate groups. Although the program has been successfully run with children in special day schools and in self-contained programs for emotionally disturbed children, it is mainly intended for at-risk youth in regular middle and high schools. The curriculum has been developed for use in ethnically diverse urban schools; however, most of the modules are appropriate for use in any secondary school setting.

Teachers, counselors, and administrators are asked to refer children for possible inclu-sion in the program. They are asked to specify the reason for referral and to include any information that would be useful for group leaders to know. Often the same child is referred by several different sources. A sample referral form is provided in Appendix A-1 and may be reproduced as is or modified to meet the needs of a particular school.

Gender and Ethnic Composition

The specifics of the composition of the groups are decided by the group leader(s), based on the needs of the students. In general, our groups have been composed of both boys and girls. There should be at least two or three members of each gender in a particular group, as it is very difficult (especially for middle-school students) to be the only girl or only boy in a group. Students who are the sole representative of their gender in a particular session have seemed ill at ease and have commented on their discomfort. More boys tend to be referred than girls, and occasionally a single-gender group may be necessary. Groups composed only of boys, especially at the middle-school level, tend to be very high energy and sometimes difficult to manage.

With regard to ethnic composition, there are pros and cons to groups containing all participants of one ethnicity. In general, groups with members of a single ethnicity, especially ethnic minorities, tend to develop trust more quickly and to disclose more deep and meaningful material earlier in the process. Drawn together by a common bond, they often share background characteristics and similar experiences that lead to greater understanding and empathy. However, some of the major elements of the program, such as discussions of ethnic pride, discrimination, and prejudice, are much more meaningful in the context of multiethnic groups. Groups with mixed ethnicity provide the opportunity for members to develop close relationships with members of other ethnic groups with whom they ordinarily would not even interact. Developed primarily in schools with significant African American and Latino populations, the SPARK groups have generally been multiethnic.

Spanish-language materials for leading groups are available in Appendixes C and D. When conducting groups in Spanish, it is important to consider the amount of student exposure to English and Spanish. For example, some students may be more comfortable speaking Spanish as they do at home, while at the same time be more familiar with written English, which they use at school. Therefore, it is important for the written material to be available in both Spanish and English, demonstrating flexibility to meet the needs of individual students. In addition, during the Ethnic Identity and Anti-Prejudice module (Module Three), Spanish-speaking groups should include discussion about students' experiences with immigration and acculturation.

Grade Level

Depending on the size of the school and the number of possible group members, grade-level distribution in the groups may vary. The smaller the range of grade levels in a particular group, the better. Developmentally, groups of sixth graders are very different from groups of ninth or 10th graders. The disparities among maturity levels can be staggering, especially in middle school as children go through puberty. We recommend that no more than two consecutive grades be lumped together. Ideally, the entry level at middle school (typically sixth grade) and at high school (usually ninth grade) would have their own groups to ease transition, and other groups could be more mixed with regard to grade level. Particularly in middle school, gender and grade

need to be considered together. For example, one group with mostly seventh-grade girls and sixth-grade boys was characterized by almost no interaction between the less mature, often silly boys and the more sophisticated girls who would not deign to relate to such "children."

Group Size

The ideal group size is between 7 and 10 members. Smaller groups do not allow for as much diversity of opinion and discussion, while larger groups do not allow time to accommodate all group members. It is best to recruit a few more group members than desired, as several may not be able to continue with the group for a variety of reasons. Common reasons for leaving the group include moving to a different district, getting expelled, not wanting to miss a class (generally physical education), and discomfort in a group setting. Especially in inner-city schools, children frequently transfer in and out of schools. Families who have been victims of community violence frequently cope by moving out of the area. Although such moves may provide more safety, they also prevent the student from utilizing the support of the group to cope with their reactions and feelings. New members can be added during the Trust Building and Communication Skills module if necessary (generally the first three sessions), but should not be added after that point, as it disrupts trust and group cohesion.

Structure of the Groups

Generally conforming to a school semester, SPARK groups are based on a 15-session model, allowing a few weeks at the beginning of each semester to recruit and interview members. The curriculum consists of seven modules. While all of the modules are usually presented, it is possible to pick and choose among them to fit the particular needs of a group or school. Similarly, the number of sessions devoted to any of the modules can be reduced or expanded to deal with hot topics or issues for a specific group of children. It is also possible to rearrange the order of the modules when appropriate. If, for example, a topic such as racial discrimination or gang involvement comes up naturally, it may be more powerful to present the module at that time, even if it is out of order. However, beginning all groups with the Trust Building and Communication Skills module (Module One) is highly recommended, since the development of a safe environment for disclosure and skills to respond empathically will facilitate the meaning and effect of the remaining modules.

Typically, groups are held during school hours and students are pulled out of a regularly scheduled class. Groups meet for one class period (generally 50 to 60 minutes) each week. In order to minimize the time away from a particular class, group sessions can alternate between two class periods. In other words, a group might meet during first period one week, during second period the next week, during first period the third week, and during second period the following week. Other means of minimizing missed class time can be worked out by individual schools. SPARK groups can be run after school as well; however, attendance tends to be much poorer, as students have other after-school activities, such as sports, and sometimes have responsibilities caring for younger siblings.

Groups have usually been held in unused classrooms or lounges. It is important for the space to be private, so that students can be assured that disclosures will remain within the group. Generally, chairs are moved to form a circle to facilitate open communication and sharing. It is helpful to have the same space for all the group sessions, if possible.

Designed to help students who may be turned off by school, SPARK groups are activity-based and interactive. Sessions begin with Check-in, where each student has the opportunity to share experiences or feelings that have occurred in the last week. Then the leader introduces the module, the goal, and the activity for the week. At the end, students participate in Check-out, where they are asked to tell what they learned from the activity to reinforce the curriculum goal, and to share their feelings about the group session.

Group Leaders

The most successful group leaders have the following qualities:

1. They really like preadolescents and adolescents.
2. They are liked by preadolescents and adolescents.
3. They can follow the curriculum but are flexible enough to accommodate a particular student's burning issue.
4. They are interested in group dynamics.
5. They are comfortable with and respect different cultures.
6. They can maintain confidentiality except where disclosure is required by law.

Group leaders who have utilized the program have generally come from within school or university settings. Leaders within school settings have generally been counselors, although interested and committed teachers can also carry out the program successfully. Leaders of other groups have been graduate students from local university training programs in clinical or educational psychology and social work.

The program works best with co-leaders, although this may not always be logistically possible. Suggested combinations would be two counselors or teachers, a counselor and a teacher, a counselor and a graduate student, or two graduate students. There are many advantages to having co-leaders. The leaders can divide such tasks as recruiting members, conducting individual pregroup (and postgroup) interviews, and getting materials photocopied and organized. Having co-leaders also provides for backup if one leader is stymied about where to take the group or if one leader is busy dealing with a difficult member. Additionally, discussing the group process with another leader often helps clarify direction and group dynamics. Co-leaders also provide more opportunity for students to bond with someone with whom they are comfortable.

Presenting the Groups to Prospective Members

Over the course of conducting groups in the past, we have found the following procedures to be most effective. They should be modified as necessary to fit the needs of a particular school and group. Students who have been referred are summoned from class in groups of about 10. To minimize stigma and address fears that they may be in trouble, students are told that teachers or counselors have identified them as students who have a lot of potential and who could work well in a group setting. The structure of the SPARK program is explained, and examples of different modules are given (see the sample script in Appendix A-2). Students who express interest are given a parent consent form, a sample of which is shown in Appendix A-3. At the end of the meeting, students are told where to return the consent forms (most commonly the counselor's office). As an incentive, they are told that they will receive a small treat, such as candy or a special pencil, when they return their consent form, regardless of whether the form has been signed. Students who have not returned their consent forms

should be contacted about one week later to see if they are still interested. If they are, they should receive another consent form. Students are told that the parent(s) can call with any questions they may have, or that the group leader will call the parent(s) if the student prefers. If a student seems interested but is not sure about the parent's response, the group leader can explicitly offer to call the parent. It is important for the person who calls to speak the same language as the parent.

Pregroup Individual Interviews and/or Questionnaires

Once parent consent forms are returned, we strongly suggest interviewing each potential group member individually if at all possible. Students who have problems in school often find completing questionnaires particularly difficult, and the results are likely to be incomplete and/or inaccurate. The pregroup interview serves several purposes:

1. *To obtain student assent.* It is important for the student to formally agree to participate in the group. It is also important to make sure the student understands the exceptions to confidentiality (if they are in danger, if they feel they may hurt themselves or someone else). A sample student assent form is included in Appendix A-4.
2. *To gather information about the student that is important for group leaders to know.* Being aware of the student's current living situation, recent stressors, feelings about education, aggression, current symptoms, exposure to violence, and feelings about gangs and drugs will greatly facilitate an understanding of what the student brings to the group. The interview also allows the leader to assess suicidality, a significant issue for some referred students that will be discussed in detail later in this chapter.

3. *To assess whether the groups have been helpful.* Gathering information about students prior to beginning the group and after it has ended allows evaluation of whether the group has been helpful.

A sample interview guide is given in Appendix A-5. Some topics covered in the interview may be irrelevant for a particular group, and leaders are urged to use only topics that seem important to assess for their own groups. Detailed information about the interview can be found in Appendix A-6. Response scales that accompany the interview are in Appendix A-7. Spanish versions of the parent consent, student assent, interview guide, and response scales are available in Appendix C.

Group Counseling Techniques

Developing Trust and Understanding Confidentiality

At the heart of any successful group intervention is the establishment of trust. This is the first task of the SPARK program and is covered in detail in Module One. At the beginning of the first session, members are asked to rate how much they trust other group members on a 5-point scale (see Appendix B-1a). This tells leaders how much of an issue trust will be in the group. Trust is often a major concern in school-based groups, since members are likely to see at least some other members in classes or on campus, may be friends (or enemies), or may have connections in the neighborhood outside of school. The Trust Building and Communication Skills module is detailed in Chapter Two.

Understanding and agreeing to confidentiality is crucial to the program. Students dis-close a great deal of personal information in the groups. It is important to provide a safe environment in which to do so and to ensure that students respect each person's right to privacy. It is a requirement of group participation that students sign the Confidentiality Contract (see Appendix B-1b) by the end of the second session. Only if members feel that what they say will be protected will they be able to make the disclosures necessary to commit to the group and its members and to receive maximum benefit from participation. To reinforce the specifics of confidentiality, members are asked to explain it in detail to latecomers or new members. The importance of signing the Confidentiality Contract cannot be underestimated. For example, before we began using formal confidentiality contracts, a girl in one group revealed that she had had an abortion. When she realized the next week that half the school now knew what she considered shameful information, she not only dropped out of the group, but also felt it necessary to change schools.

Building Group Cohesion

In addition to building trust, the program uses several other mechanisms to develop a sense of group cohesion. Specific methods for implementing the following are given in Chapter Two in the Trust Building and Communication Skills module.

Group Name

In the first session, a list of possible group names is generated by the group and voted on. Having a mutually agreed-upon name, no matter how strange, allows for a sense of belonging. Names have included "Yo Mama," "Killer Bees," "The Confidentiality Club," and "Bruins [UCLA team name] and Buttheads."

Group-Generated Rules and Consequences

Group rules are generated by members when they become necessary, both to enhance group cohesion and to set a procedure for keeping order that works for youth who may frequently rebel against rules and authority. The younger the group members, the sooner group rules may need to be developed. They are almost always necessary in middle-school groups by Session Two, but they may not be needed until quite late in the curriculum (or not at all) for older high-school students. Group leaders write down all suggested rules, whether appropriate or not (some interesting initial suggestions have been "Bring gum to share with all members" and "Everyone must wear black shoes"), ask for opinions and discussion, and then have members vote on each one. If the leader feels that a particular rule is needed after the group generates their list or at another time, he or she can ask, for example, "Do we need a rule about hitting other people?" Generally, the group will agree, but the leader will not impose a rule unilaterally, except under extreme circumstances.

Some typical rules a group might develop include:

1. Don't touch anyone else or their things.
2. No name calling.
3. Don't interrupt when someone else is talking.
4. Respect other people's feelings.
5. No eating unless you share with all the group members.

After the rules are generated, the group also generates the consequences for not following the rules. Leaders ask, "What should happen if one of these rules is broken?" Members generate a list of possible consequences, and leaders again write down all suggestions for later discussion. If a really in-

appropriate consequence is suggested (e.g., beat up the rule violator), members will usually nix it during the discussion period. If they do not, the leader can ask, "Does anyone see any possible problems with this one?" After full discussion, consequences are voted on. Ideal consequences are usually a warning, followed by one or two time-outs (for a specified period of time) in the room, and then by sending the student back to class for the rest of the session. Groups do not always generate these ideal consequences, but the ones they develop almost always work as long as they are clearly enforced. Some of the more unique consequences that groups have developed include doing push-ups, writing standards, and sitting in the corner facing the wall. The final list of group rules and consequences should be posted so that it is available during all future group sessions.

In addition to being developed by the group, rules and consequences are also enforced by the group. If no one calls a rule that is being broken, the leader will ask, "Does anyone see a rule being broken?" Almost always, a member will identify the rule. If not, the leader can say, for example, "What about the 'no interrupting' rule?" Allowing group members to generate and enforce the rules gives them a sense of ownership and cohesion with regard to the group process, and it facilitates the internalization of limits and consequences for their behavior.

Emphasizing Commonalities and Eliciting Support

Another avenue for building group cohesion is helping members see commonalities among their lives and their troublesome issues. The first Trust Building and Communication Skills session involves an exercise for pointing out similarities among group members (the Me Too game in Session One). In addition, group leaders comment on areas where group members may have interests or situations in common. One way to accomplish this is by asking questions—for example, "Has anyone else's parents gone through a divorce?" or "Are there others who have to take care of their younger brothers or sisters?" Another technique is to bring up previously disclosed statements that relate to the current discussion—for instance, "Jose, you told us a few weeks ago about your cousin's being shot. Did you have some of the same feelings that Gina is describing?"

Empathic Responding and Reflections

In order for group members to feel comfortable and free to talk about difficult things, an atmosphere where such sensitive disclosures are treated with respect is needed. The first step, building trust, was discussed previously. However, once trust is established and disclosures begin, the manner in which they are handled will determine whether the process of self-disclosure is enhanced or diminished. Deep disclosures about topics such as the student's family or inner feelings make most adolescents uncomfortable, and some almost instinctively respond by making a joke out of it, changing the subject, or belittling or doubting the disclosure. We use four ways to help group members develop an empathic and respectful way of responding to the sensitive disclosures of other group members. First, group leaders model understanding and empathic responses to members' sensitive disclosures, mainly using reflection of feelings—for example, "You must have felt devastated when you learned that your sister had run away" or "Sounds like you were really mad when he threw the ball directly at your face." Second, as part of the Trust Building and Communication Skills module, group members participate in one activity to help them rec-

ognize and label feelings (Feelings Grab Bag) and another that gives them the opportunity to respond with empathy to the anonymous disclosures of other group members (Secret Pooling). Third, the Helping Responses handout in Session Three of the Trust Building and Communication Skills module gives explicit instructions about responding in helpful ways to others' disclosures. Fourth, leaders ask members to tell how they think another feels—for example, "What do you think Sarah might be feeling in response to the insult from her teacher?" —or how they would feel if it happened to them—"How do you think you would feel if a teacher said that to you?" Usually, not all members fully reach the goal of empathic responding; however, if most group members learn to treat sensitive disclosures with respect, an atmosphere of trust can be maintained even if one or two members continue to respond somewhat inappropriately.

Group Process

Reflections of Group Process

In a manner similar to that discussed above for reflecting the feelings of group members, leaders also reflect the tenor or tone of the entire group. This is particularly helpful when feelings in the group are intense, when strong feelings may have developed between group members, or when there is a breakdown in the group process. Examples of group process reflections are: "I notice that everyone got silly and giggly when John mentioned sex with his girlfriend"; "Group members seem to be feeling a lot of rage about Jessica's being beaten up by a gang"; "Right now, it seems as if people's race is motivating which side they are on, rather than being able to work things out as a group"; or "What Sammy said was so heavy that it's hard for people to respond, even though I can see from your faces that you have lots of reactions."

Pointing Out Verbal versus Nonverbal Communication

It is also useful to note instances in which what the student says does not match how he or she says it. For example, if a student talks about having a great time with his friends but does so in a low voice with no expression, the leader might say, "Your words say that you had a fantastic time, but your voice and how you are sitting say something very different." This commonly comes up when a member is nervous about talking about something upsetting. A student might disclose that she was betrayed by her best friend in a hurtful way, but she may smile and laugh as she discloses the betrayal. The leader can point out the discrepancy between the verbal and nonverbal communication by saying something like "You are telling us about something that seems hurtful and sad, yet you are smiling and laughing. Maybe it's really painful to actually feel the sad feelings." Sometimes group members will point out such discrepancies, although they may do it in nonsupportive ways. For example, a student may say, "Oh, you're not bothered by being jumped after school—you're laughing about it. Maybe it didn't even really happen." The group leader can help by pointing out the discrepancy: "You're wondering if Maria could have been jumped because you think she would be feeling upset and she's telling us about it while laughing. Maria, maybe it's easier to share what happened if you put away your sad and mad feelings and make a joke about it."

Processing Interpersonal Issues between Group Members

If interpersonal issues arise between two group members based on interactions in the

group, students are encouraged to share their feelings with each other and to state what they would like from the other person. For example, a student might say, "I was really pissed when you called me a fat pig, and I'd like you to stop calling me names." If a student is unable to share feelings or state what he or she would like, other group members are asked to help. The group leader might ask, "Who thinks they know how Joe might be feeling now?" or "What could Tony do to help Gina feel better right now?" or "What can we say to Gina or to Tony to let them know we understand how they feel?"

Because the program is generally school-based, some of the members often have other relationships (friends, enemies, neighbors, etc.) that predate the start of the group. That they could continue to interact with each other provides the possibility of ongoing support after the end of the SPARK program, but it also has the potential of creating difficulties in the group. Over the years, we have found that it is best not to spend too much group time trying to process and deal with anger or rivalry between group members that developed long before the group began meeting. Doing so can take time away from important material in the curriculum. In our experience, these long-standing issues are not easily resolved. In addition, focusing much group time and energy on two students may be detrimental to the other group members. Generally, it is helpful to briefly air the issues to see if any solution is immediately apparent. If not, we have found it best to physically separate enemies so that they do not sit near each other, and to suggest that they deal with their outside issues away from the group.

Occasionally one group member will start to like another group member romantically. If the student's ardor is not returned, the leader may need to help the other student tell the Lothario to back off. For example, if a student looks uncomfortable when the admirer sits too close or physically touches him or her, the leader can ask the student if he or she is comfortable with Pat sitting so close, and if the answer is no, the student can be encouraged to ask Pat to move back. Sometimes the attraction is mutual. If there is overt affection or if the talking between the two becomes distracting to the group, the rules can be invoked or the students can be asked to separate so that everyone can concentrate on the group.

Developmental Considerations

Maturity level and relevant issues vary greatly over the secondary school age range. Younger children are affected differently by exposure to family and community violence than older teens. They show more fear, more intrusive and disturbing thoughts, and fewer coping skills than older victims and witnesses. Older teens exposed to violence tend to be more flat in their affect, and it sometimes seems as if they have become numb as a defense against their horrific experiences. One 10th grader exposed to both community and family violence described how he felt nothing most of the time; the only time he really felt alive was when he and his friends lobbed cherry bombs at cars and watched the explosions. So while younger children need help learning how to contain and appropriately channel their affect, some older teens need to focus on exploration and expression of feelings. It can also help to normalize these reactions in the group, stressing that what may seem like an insensitive reaction or an overreaction to a particular event may represent a useful coping mechanism in the face of repeated exposure to adversity.

Preteens and young teens need more structure in their groups than do older teens. Middle-school group leaders need to stick closely to the curriculum and the ac-

tivities, develop rules, and make sure the group enforces the rules strictly. In contrast, in most older high-school groups, leaders can allow a discussion relevant to the topic that is not in the curriculum and then easily relate it back to the main curricular points.

Maintaining Order and Leader Sanity

The generation of group rules and consequences provides the basis for maintaining enough order for students to profit from the curriculum (see Chapter Two, Module One, Session Two for an in-depth discussion about establishing group rules). Many of the children referred for groups, particularly in inner-city schools, have strong negative feelings about authority figures and actively seek to undermine them. Putting the onus of developing and enforcing the group rules on the group members helps the students take ownership of the group and reduces disruption. However, the leaders must provide the parameters to allow this approach to be successful. The two most common leader errors in maintaining order are that (1) leaders enforce the rules themselves, which sets up an "us–them" relationship similar to that which many students experience with their parents or teachers, and (2) leaders want to be "nice guys" and therefore ignore or gloss over minor rule violations, which often results in things getting out of hand very quickly.

The most effective leader stance is to be clear and firm in *facilitating* enforcement of the rules. That means that if members do not call a rule that is being broken, the leader asks if anyone sees a rule being broken. If no one answers (which is rare), the leader wonders aloud about the particular rule—for example, "What about number 3, no name calling?" Similarly, the leader must make sure that the consequence ensues, but the leader does not directly impose it. Instead the leader asks, "What is the consequence?" and group members state the consequence for the rule violator—for example, "Shanika, you need to sit in the corner for 5 minutes without saying anything." It is extremely important to establish an expectation that the rules and consequences, once needed and devised by the group, will be followed.

In general, expect younger adolescent groups to require more management, earlier rule generation, and more rule enforcement than older groups. Sixth-grade boys usually require the most containment. In younger groups and in the occasional older group with management issues, leaders have found it helpful to use a group reward at the end of the session. Members usually get one small piece of candy if they have had no more than one warning and two pieces if they have not had any warnings.

Uses and Parameters of Check-In and Check-Out

Check-in occurs at the beginning of every group after the first meeting, and each student is encouraged to contribute. It is meant to help members reconnect and to give them an opportunity to bring up things that are happening in their lives that might need to be discussed in the group. For example, if a family member has been hurt, a girlfriend or boyfriend is seeing someone else, or a fight is brewing in the school, students have an opportunity to share and to receive support from the other members. Leaders both model empathic reflections and positively comment on the empathic statements or self-disclosures of others. In addition, leaders may have to cut off some students who feel compelled to share every detail of their weekend, as well as deal with inappropriate laughter or comments that may not help the discloser feel safe.

This is usually done either by asking if a rule is being broken (such as "respecting others" or "no interrupting") or by using group process techniques. The leader can ask other members how they would feel if they were talking about something very difficult and people laughed or made fun of them, or can comment on how uncomfortable the student must have been that he or she needed to put down the discloser.

Similarly, Check-out occurs at the end of each meeting. There are three purposes to Check-out. First, it allows group members to share how they felt about the activity and the topic of the day's group. Second, it allows members to give feedback to each other (e.g., "I sure hope your brother is OK" or "I hope you find your backpack"). Third, it allows the leader to make sure that the point of the activity and lesson were learned. The leader asks: "What was the point of the activity today? What did you learn? How might you apply this in your life this week?" This reinforces the lesson and encourages generalization. Specific questions are given in the Check-out section for each session of the curriculum.

Check-in and Check-out can also be utilized by group leaders to reinforce points made in previous sessions. This is probably most commonly done with Hot-Head and Cool-Head responses (from the Anger Management and Problem-Solving Skills module) when students bring up incidents involving aggression or violence. However, it is helpful to use relevant information from any previous module in Check-in or Check-out to emphasize transfer and generalization of points discussed.

Issues in Ending the Groups

Many students grow attached to the leaders and other members of their group. Therefore, it is important to let them know when the end of the group is approaching to allow members to talk about their feelings about ending. Feelings of sadness or abandonment, which may be intensified by the students' own previous personal experiences with loss, need to be expressed and discussed. We suggest bringing it up with about four sessions left, at first simply pointing out the number of sessions remaining. In the next three weeks, it is important to mention the number of sessions remaining, and elicit the feelings that members have about the group ending. Check-in and Check-out provide the best mechanism for discussing these feelings. Specific ways of bringing up and discussing the end of the group are given in the curriculum in the relevant sessions.

The importance of dealing with students' feelings about ending the groups was most poignantly brought home by our most difficult experience with ending a group. When we were first doing SPARK groups, we worked with a very needy group of students, many of whom did not live with their own parents. At that point, we were running 10-week groups, and the leaders were not focused on how important they had become to these children or how termination might affect the members. However, when it was time to leave after the 10th session, several children ran out to the street and laid down in front of the leaders' car to prevent them from leaving. The leaders were terribly upset and felt distressed for the students.

Often, group leaders also experience sadness in anticipation of finishing the group, and we encourage the leaders to share these feelings with the group. In addition to modeling expressing in-group emotions, it also provides the opportunity to genuinely express feelings. Of course, occasionally there are groups that are so difficult to manage that the leaders may welcome the end. In general, the amount of emotional connection between leaders and students deter-

mines how strong the leaders' feelings about ending the groups will be.

Specific activities for the last session are detailed in the curriculum. A party with snacks is held. Members are asked to reflect back on what was covered in the group meetings and what they will take from the groups to help them in their lives. In addition, students participate in a group feedback exercise (What I Like about You, see Appendix B-7a) where each person tells what he or she values in each group member, and the group leader writes these down for the students to take with them. Each member also receives a Certificate of Achievement for completing the SPARK program (an example of this certificate appears in Appendix B-7b).

Sometimes groups may want to continue or to have reunions after the sessions have ended. In our program, we have not been able to continue because other students are waiting to participate in SPARK groups. However, if the school has the resources for continuing the groups with a less-structured format, and if the leaders feel it would be productive, continuing could be highly beneficial. We have occasionally held reunions (usually toward the end of the next semester or at the beginning of the next school year), which students have enjoyed. This provides the chance to reinforce curricular points (often relating to anger management or conflict resolution) in addition to allowing students to renew relationships and catch up on each other's lives.

Dilemmas for Group Leaders

Handling Issues of Child Abuse and Suicidality

Child abuse and suicidality are difficult issues. We have found that they come up with some frequency for at-risk adolescents.

They can arise either in the pregroup interviews or during the group sessions themselves. The first and basic principle is to discuss exceptions to confidentiality right at the beginning of the interview and to cover this in detail as part of the confidentiality discussion in the first group session. Adolescents who then choose to share such experiences and feelings are aware that the material cannot be kept confidential. We focus these initial discussions on the need to keep the child safe.

Child Abuse

When physical or sexual abuse is disclosed by adolescents, it must be reported to the appropriate authorities (generally the Department of Children's Services if the perpetrator is a family member, or the local police if the perpetrator is not a family member, although specific procedures may vary from state to state). We have found it most useful for the group leader to stay with the student throughout the reporting process, even if the leader is not typically the person who makes child abuse reports in a particular school or setting. The leader's role is to offer support to the student and to explore his or her feelings about disclosure, including fear of consequences or reprisal. We suggest that whoever typically makes child abuse reports in the school make any reports that come up in the context of the program; this arrangement and specific procedures should be clarified before the beginning of groups. When groups have been led by university graduate students, the university student has taken the adolescent to the appropriate school reporter and remained with the student throughout the reporting procedure.

It is helpful and supportive to check with the student within the next day or so after the report has been made. The leader should elicit and process the student's feelings, discuss what may have happened with the social service agency or police, and help the student cope with any consequences he or she may have experienced with regard to the family's reaction. Sometimes it is helpful to offer to meet with the student and the student's family.

Suicidality

Suicidal thoughts are reported even more frequently than child abuse by adolescents referred for SPARK groups. In our pregroup interview, we ask students to rate how often a variety of things happen to them. When a student answers "sometimes," "lots of times," or "all the time" to "wanting to hurt yourself" or "wanting to kill yourself," we follow up at the end of the interview to assess the seriousness of the statement. There is more reason for concern if (1) the student has made a previous suicide attempt or (2) the child has a well-formulated plan and the means to carry out that plan (e.g., it would be much more serious for a student to plan to jump off a tall building if the student lived in Manhattan than if he or she lived in a small rural community). For a student who has suicidal thoughts but is not judged a significant risk, the group leader contracts with the student not to take any action without talking with the group leader first and lets the student know how to reach her or him if the student feels as if he or she might attempt suicide. Often this provides an opportunity for a student to talk about a significant life crisis or circumstance. Additionally, we encourage students to use available social support by helping them identify at least one person with whom they can talk if they are feeling distressed.

If the student is unable to make such a contract or if the risk of suicide is seen as substantial, the parent or guardian is contacted by the leader (or other appropriate school personnel). The leader should be able to recommend resources for individual counseling to the parent. It should be explained to the student that contacting the parent is necessary in order to keep the student safe. Sometimes students express fear that they will get into trouble if their parents find out about their suicidal feelings. Sometimes they also feel shame or guilt about their suicidal feelings. The group leader should take care in addressing these concerns. It can help to explain to both students and parents that it is not uncommon for adolescents to have suicidal thoughts or feelings sometimes, and to praise the students for sharing these feelings so they can be safe and get help.

Balancing the Needs of Individual Group Members with the Requirements of the Psychoeducational Curriculum

A common problem that arises is how to balance presenting the information and activities in the curriculum with the needs of individual group members. If, for example, a problem that a student brings up in Check-in takes more than half of the session to discuss, the activity for the day may not be completed, and the important points in that session may not be made. If the leader has the luxury of extending the number of sessions of the group, this is a less serious issue than it is when the group needs to be finished at a certain time. This has been most problematic at schools that operate year-round. In these schools, semesters may be shorter and may be followed by long breaks, making it imperative to follow the curriculum closely so that all relevant modules can be presented in a timely fashion.

One way of dealing with this dilemma is to develop a sense of what types of student issues are important enough to warrant time

that would otherwise go to the curriculum. One such issue is current loss. If a student has lost someone in the last month through death or if a loved one has been seriously injured or ill, the student needs the support of the group. Similarly, if the student has been seriously hurt or has experienced a traumatic event in the last month, or if a serious fight or disruption at the school has occurred, significant discussion in the group is warranted.

There are several types of situations about which students may want to talk at length at Check-in, but they need to be contained so that the group can proceed with the curricular activities. Some group members like to share every detail of their weekend or may want to talk about teachers and other students who bother them. These issues do not deserve attention to the detriment of the curriculum, and students should be politely discouraged from talking too much. For example, the group leader might say, "Thanks for sharing about your weekend, Hakim. Let's move on to Cindy."

Another situation that can cause concern for the leader occurs when a very troubled student makes long and disturbing disclosures week after week. If, for example, a suicidal student with many family problems talks for a long time in every group about these issues, the other members can become focused on helping the student, making it a therapy group for that student, or they may begin to ostracize the student as weird or engage in teasing. If it becomes clear that this is a pattern in the group, it is helpful for the leader to meet individually with the student and make a referral for individual or family counseling. In this case, the student's issues are too major to be resolved in the group, and they take time that is needed to help all the students with the shared issues raised in the curriculum.

Dealing with Members Who Do Not Participate

Students who do not participate pose a dilemma for leaders. If students are not encouraged to participate, they will not receive maximum benefit. On the other hand, if students are pushed too hard, they may feel uncomfortable and drop out. We use multiple approaches to help such students become part of the group. First, we actively encourage them to engage in the activities. For example, in the first session, if a student is not participating in the Me Too game, the leader will name something he or she has in common with the student that should make the student stand up (e.g., "I'm wearing black shoes" or "I have brown eyes."). In later sessions, this would involve asking the student, if appropriate, "Has this ever happened to you?"

Second, group leaders make comments that convey group interest, support, and acceptance. Examples include: "You don't have to talk about this now, but when you're ready, we'd really like to hear about your experience" and "I bet everyone here has had times when they felt like nobody could possibly understand how they felt and when they didn't want to talk about something, but sometimes it really can help to share and talk." The goal is to convey support without pushing the student.

Third, if conveying support does not elicit participation after several sessions, we wonder aloud whether something is making it hard for the student to participate. If the student in question does not answer, the other group members can be asked if they have any ideas about why it might be hard for the student to participate. Sometimes other students can give very insightful answers, such as "I don't think he feels comfortable speaking English"; "Terry and Bruce make fun of him whenever he opens his mouth, so I understand why he wouldn't

feel safe to talk here"; or "He doesn't ever talk in class either, but he talks fine when he's with his friends." Such answers may provide the basis for making adjustments in the group so that the member feels safe.

Fourth, if the student continues to be withdrawn and noncommunicative by the end of the third session, the leader may need to speak with the student individually about whether he or she wants to continue coming to the group. If the student does want to continue, he or she is encouraged to participate in the activities at least minimally. In other words, if each member is to take a turn in an activity, the member should be willing to speak, even if only short or minimal answers are given and no information is volunteered. The leader continues to encourage participation but does not force it. Occasionally, the group leader may ask the student whether he or she would like to share feelings about the topic, but the student's refusal should be accepted. If the student feels so uncomfortable about sharing that he or she does not wish to remain in the group, the group leader should accept the decision and help the student feel comfortable about stopping.

Dealing with Chronically Disruptive Members

Occasionally, a group will have a charismatic student who is highly disruptive during a number of sessions. Such members have the potential to ruin a group, but they can also be a positive force and a source of great energy. First, the student's behavior is dealt with, using the rules and consequences. If this is unsuccessful in ending the student's disruption of the group, the student may be a candidate for the "leader talk," which can result in channeling the student's energy for the benefit of the group process. In addition to being disruptive, candidates for the leader talk must be well-liked or respected by other students. Strange or universally disliked students are not candidates. In the leader talk, a group leader meets individually with the disruptive student with the following goals:

1. To acknowledge how powerful the student is—the leader might say, "The other group members look up to you and want to be like you."
2. To note the difficulties the group is experiencing—"You know things haven't been going too smoothly in the group, with people interrupting while others are talking. We're not able to do the activities, and everyone ends up frustrated."
3. To enlist the student's help in getting the group under control—"I was wondering if you might be able to help, since you are a natural leader and the kids listen to you and think you're cool. You could act like kind of a co-leader and help keep the group focused on the activities and not be so rowdy. What do you think?"

Generally, the student is flattered, puffs up with pride, and agrees to help out. Then at the beginning of the next group session, the leader reminds the student privately, "So you're going to help out today, right?" If the student is less disruptive, the leader thanks the student privately for the help at the end of the session and expresses hope that the student will be willing to continue helping, since the group went so much better today. This manner of dealing with chronically disruptive members has generally been very successful.

Parameters of the Group Leader Role

Participation in Activities

The leader begins the first activity, the Me Too game, and needs to participate in order to model disclosure and encourage participation by all group members. How much the group leader participates in the other activities depends on the tenor of the particular group and the group leader's comfort level. In some groups, members will press the group leaders to participate in activities such as Feelings Grab Bag, Labeling, and Hot-Head Cool-Head role play. In these cases, it is helpful for the group leader to participate, since as the members may be asking the leader to take the same risks they are taking. This tends to increase trust in the group. However, if there is an activity that the leader does not feel comfortable participating in, then the leader should tell the group. A stream of questions asking why and cajoling may follow. For other groups, leader participation may not be an issue at all, and leaders will not be asked to participate if they do not naturally do so.

Self-Disclosure by Leaders

Similarly, groups vary in the degree to which they press leaders to disclose details of their lives or their feelings or opinions, and leaders vary in their comfort in sharing such information. As discussed above, sometimes pressing leaders to tell about themselves is a test of trust. Leaders are asking members to share difficult feelings and events—will the leaders be willing to do the same? Most frequently, leaders are asked about whether they have a boyfriend, girlfriend, husband, or wife. Other common questions involve children, what the leaders did last weekend or last summer, and where they went to college. The most difficult questions that leaders are frequently asked relate to sex and drug use. For example, leaders have been asked, "Do you and your boyfriend have sex?" "Have you ever smoked pot?" and "What drugs did you do in high school and college?" The rule of thumb about leader comfort in answering applies here as well, but the issues are more complex.

In general, leaders have to decide whether they are willing to honestly disclose their own experiences when they may run counter to what they are hoping to teach the students. The three possible responses a leader has to such questions are to (1) honestly disclose his or her experiences; (2) say that it is personal or that he or she doesn't feel comfortable talking about it; or (3) lie and give the answer that reflects the value he or she is trying to communicate to the group. Each of these options is fraught with possible negative consequences. If a leader is honest and, for example, discloses that he or she smoked pot, the leader may gain the trust of group members but could be at risk if members violate the Confidentiality Contract and let other school personnel or their parents know that the leader used illegal drugs. If a leader lets the group know that he or she is not comfortable sharing with them, the leader is being honest, but may be sending the message that it is not safe to disclose in the group, and the level of openness may drop. If the leader lies about experiences, the leader communicates the message to the group but may feel dishonest and may be perceived as such by group members. Obviously, there are no easy answers; leaders should be prepared for such dilemmas and think about their feelings prior to starting work with the group. It is important not to do so much disclosure that the leader becomes a group member rather than the group leader and facilitator.

Dealing with One's Own Feelings

As leaders come to know the group members intimately and in depth, a variety of feelings may be stimulated. In our experience, the most common feelings that cause

leaders distress are rescue fantasies and frustration. Certain students with negative past experiences elicit strong empathic feelings in therapists—for example, a student witnessed his father shoot and kill his mother; other students have lost relatives to community violence; and many students relate instances of emotional abuse or neglect by parents or other caregivers. It is helpful to make referrals for individual or family counseling where appropriate and to be empathic, available, and understanding with the student. But it is also important to recognize limits. The leader cannot take the student home or become a substitute parent.

The other common distressing feeling of group leaders is frustration. A common source of frustration is not being able to reach a student. This happens most frequently when students appear to have great potential but keep sabotaging themselves, for example by not studying for a test or by fighting after committing to avoid fights. The other common source of frustration is students who undermine or disrupt the group. Techniques for handling such students are discussed above, but leaders also need to deal with their own feelings of anger and irritation at such students. Frequently, disruptive students have had major losses and painful experiences in their lives. It can be helpful for the leader to reinterpret the student's behavior as an expression of underlying distress, which generally allows the leader to feel more connected and less angry.

In general, the feelings of group leaders toward most members become positive and deepen over the course of the group. Leaders have generally found the SPARK group counseling experience to be challenging, enriching, exciting, and meaningful as they affect the lives of youth.

CHAPTER TWO

The SPARK Curriculum

The SPARK curriculum combines a group process model aimed at developing interpersonal skills and a psychoeducational model focused on building competence by development of specific skills needed by all youth, especially those at high risk. The goal of the first module of the curriculum, Trust Building and Communication Skills, is to develop an atmosphere of increasing trust to set the stage for supportive interactions, meaningful self-disclosure, and respectful problem-solving. In addition, throughout the curriculum, the group process orientation can be seen in the emphasis on discussing difficult interactions, developing a group identity, using the group-generated rules and consequences, and focusing on supportive, affirming responding.

The choice of the curriculum content after Module One is based on a psychoeducational model aimed at developing skills to alleviate common problems for high-risk youth. It begins with a module on Anger Management and Problem-Solving Skills in order to build a framework and a set of skills for dealing with a variety of issues that are faced by today's youth, issues that are discussed in later modules. The anger management and problem-solving techniques advocated in this module are brought up, emphasized, and reinforced throughout the rest of the curriculum to continue and expand skill building. The other modules were selected because they represent areas of significant concern for at-risk youth. Middle-school and junior high years are crucial turning points for academic achievement, with many students beginning to fail, lose motivation, and earn poor grades in a downward spiral with deleterious consequences. Therefore, a module that focuses on educational aspirations, how to reach career goals, and the importance of developing study skills now seems essential. Similarly, peer pressure around a variety of areas, such as drugs, gangs, and sex, represents a serious challenge for at-risk youth and needs to be addressed. For all students, and especially those living in multiethnic communities, exploration of ethnic identity, stereotypes, prejudice, and discrimination is necessary. In addition, application of problem-solving skills to complicated or disrupted family relationships is needed, as well as a focus on how parents can be a resource. Examination of community violence and posttraumatic stress reactions is part of the curriculum because this is a pervasive aspect of life for most inner-city children.

The SPARK curriculum consists of seven modules. Although generally used in its entirety, it is possible to select specific modules that would be especially useful for a particular group of students. If only selected modules are used, we suggest that all concepts and sessions in the particular module be presented. Modules can also be expanded to more sessions for specific issues that may require more time and care. For example, in a school setting with a great deal of racial tension, the Ethnic Identity and Anti-prejudice module might be expanded, with more opportunities for discussion and personalization to the particular school's situation. Similarly, for a group of especially aggressive students, the Anger Management and Problem-Solving Skills module might be expanded from two to four sessions to allow for more practice of skills. If exposure to violence is not an issue in a particular community, the Exposure to Violence and Posttraumatic Stress Reactions module can be omitted, although the first session is useful in exploring student's scary experiences of all kinds.

Overview of Module Content

Module One: Trust Building
and Communication Skills

■ Three sessions help students learn to trust each other, listen empathically, feel ownership of the group, and share their feelings.

Module Two: Anger Management
and Problem-Solving Skills

■ Two or three sessions help students learn to generate and practice alternatives to violence in dealing with anger and provocation.

Module Three: Ethnic Identity
and Anti-Prejudice

■ Three sessions help students develop positive feelings of ethnic pride, address and discuss prejudice, and understand and accept people from other ethnic groups.

Module Four: Educational Aspirations

■ Three sessions, one of which is a field trip to a local university, help students set high but reasonable educational aspirations, address barriers to academic success, and identify specific steps they can take toward doing better in school.

Module Five: Peer Pressure and Gangs

■ Two sessions help students generate and practice alternatives to giving in to peer pressure and discuss alternatives to gang involvement.

Module Six: Exposure to Violence
and Posttraumatic Stress Reactions

■ One or two sessions help students discuss and understand their emotional reactions to witnessing or being the victims of violence.

Module Seven: Family Relationships

■ One or two sessions help students understand and accept their families and those traits in themselves that are similar to family members—traits they like and those they wish were different.

Recruitment Criteria

Students appropriate for the SPARK program

1. Currently experience academic, social, emotional, and/or family difficulties or have been exposed to high levels of violence.
2. Can work cooperatively in a group.
3. Attend school regularly.
4. Show interest in participating in the program.
5. Can miss one class period per week.
6. Do not display high levels of disruptive behavior.

See Chapter One for additional discussion of recruitment criteria.

Trust Building and Communication Skills

Goal To help students learn to trust each other, listen empathically, feel owner-ship of the group, and share their feelings

Overview of Sessions

Session One
- *Purpose:* Develop process skills: cooperation, group cohesion, self-disclosure, universality of experience
- *Content:* (1) Discussion of confidentiality, (2) Me Too game, (3) selection of group name

Session Two
- *Purpose:* Develop process skills: group cohesion, group owner-ship, empathic responding, identifying and sharing feelings
- *Content:* (1) Selection of group rules, (2) Feelings Grab Bag

Session Three
- *Purpose:* Develop process skills: self-disclosure, empathic respond-ing, universality of experience
- *Content:* Secret Pooling

Session One

Activities
- ✔ Trust ratings and introduction
- ✔ Discussion of confidentiality
- ✔ Discussion of member selection
- ✔ Me Too game
- ✔ Selection of group name
- ✔ Check-out

Materials
- ✔ Curriculum
- ✔ Trust ratings (one copy for each student—see Appendix B-1a)
- ✔ Name tags
- ✔ Confidentiality Contracts (one copy for each student—see Appendix B-1b)
- ✔ Masking tape
- ✔ A pad of paper large enough to be seen by all students
- ✔ Brightly colored pens for writing on the pad of paper

Content

Pregroup Trust Ratings and Introduction

As students come in, ask them to fill out pregroup trust ratings. Say, **"Please fill out these sheets. We use these to check whether we need to do more to help build trust in the group. We will be asking you to complete these ratings again in a couple of weeks."**

1. Ask each student to write his or her name on a name tag.

2. Introduce leaders. Give name, background, and other information you feel would be useful.

3. Describe the group.

   a. Practical issues: dates and times (explain that the group will last 15 weeks).

   b. Overview of content: Say, **"We have different topics we will cover in the groups. For each topic, we will spend part of the time doing some fun activities and part of the time discussing your opinions and feelings about the topics."**

   c. Group goals: **"We want this to be a place where we can all feel safe to talk about things that are important to us."**

Confidentiality Contracts

It is important to discuss confidentiality in great detail because the success of the group depends on group members' keeping confidentiality. Breaking of confidentiality can have severe consequences for individuals in the group.

1. Pass out the contracts and say, **"Don't sign these yet. Confidentiality is very important, and we want to make sure you think about this carefully before signing these contracts."**

2. Discuss the meaning of confidentiality: **"In a group like this, it is important to have complete confidentiality. Who can tell me what confidentiality means?"** Solicit responses. To reinforce responding, after each response make a

motion or sound of approval, such as **"um-hm."** After hearing a nearly correct response, say, **"Right, so, in a nutshell, confidentiality means that nothing that is said in this room goes outside of the room."**

3. Discuss the importance of confidentiality: **"Can anyone tell me why this might be important?"** If no one can, prompt by asking, **"Imagine that you brought up something very important in the group. Then during the next week somebody in the group tells their friend what you said. Pretty soon, many people know what you said. How would you feel about talking in the group next week?"** Students will probably say that they would not feel like sharing.

4. Discuss the difficulty of confidentiality: **"Sometimes this can be really hard. One time when you might be tempted to break confidentiality is if you are talking to a person in this room when other people are around. Remember, you can't talk about what the person said in here. Or if you're talking to your best friend, you can't tell him or her what another person said here."**

5. Discuss the limits to confidentiality: **"I also will keep everything that you say in here confidential. That means I will not tell anyone what you say in here. Now there is one time when I will not be able to keep confidentiality. That is if I have reason to think that you or someone else is in danger—for example, if you tell us someone is hitting you or that you are thinking of hurting yourself or someone else. In that case, we will have to tell someone else what you said. This is because our first concern is your safety, and we need to make sure that you are safe. However, anything else you say in here will be kept confidential."** (If you are the person at your school who is the designated reporter for child abuse, you may want to modify the preceding statement to reflect that you will need to take the steps required to make sure the child is safe.)

6. Reading and signing of the contracts: **"Now let's read the contract carefully. Each student can read one sentence. Who wants to start?"** After the contract has been read completely, give an opportunity for students to ask questions. Then say, **"Now think about this carefully. If you feel ready to sign a contract saying that you will keep everything said in the group confidential, please sign. If you are not sure, please think it over this week and sign the contract next week if you decide that you are willing to keep the group discussion confidential."**

7. A good way to reinforce confidentiality is to have group members teach other members what confidentiality means. For example, if a student arrives late for the group or misses the first week, you can have another group member explain to the newcomer what confidentiality means, and you can correct any misconceptions. Sometimes there are many students arriving late or missing the first week so that the students actually hear confidentiality explained four or five times by the end of the Trust Building and Communication Skills module.

Why Students Were Selected for the Group

Explore participant reactions to being selected for the group. Begin to explore feelings about trusting other members in this setting. Many group members may fear that this will be a stigmatizing experience or that it means that they are bad.

1. As the program becomes established in the school and students hear that the groups are fun, this fear will be easier to overcome.

2. Explain that **"Almost all students will have various problems at different times. We chose you not because you were having problems, but because someone, either a teacher or a counselor, thought that you would be able to make the most of this type of experience. Some students can't work together in groups very well, but someone in the school thought you would be able to get along and work well with the other group members."**

Trust Building Activity: Me Too Game

This is a game similar to musical chairs. The goal of the game is for students to say something about themselves that they think other people will have in common with them. It encourages self-disclosure, creates a feeling of universality, and helps build group cohesion. This game provides a good opportunity for leaders to bond with the group. Try to laugh a lot and keep a light atmosphere. It is important to have a good time with the group and help them enjoy being part of the group.

1. Place chairs in the shape of a horseshoe, with one fewer chair than there are group members. Put a line of masking tape in the front of the horseshoe to mark the "it" zone, the line behind which everyone has to stand until the "it" person finds a seat.

2. Say, **"We're going to play a game called the Me Too game. One person stands in the empty space at the front of the horseshoe. The person says his or her name and something about himself or herself, such as shoe size, favorite color or movie, or feelings, like about homework or family. Then everyone else who has that thing in common with the person standing has to stand, come to the front of the horseshoe, wait for the 'it' person to sit, then scramble for the remaining chairs. Make sure you don't push anyone. The person left standing becomes 'it' and now has to say something about himself or herself. Let's try it. I'll be 'it' first."**

3. Say your name and something about yourself that you think others will have in common. Then ask, **"Is that true for anyone else? OK, everyone else who has that in common with me has to come up here, stand behind the tape, and wait until I find a seat."**

4. Sit down and remind students to find a seat once you are seated. Say, **"OK, looks like [student who is left standing] is 'it.' [Student], say your name and something about yourself."**

5. It helps to model increasingly personal disclosures as the game progresses, such as "I get mad at my mom sometimes" or "I wish I were a better student."

6. If there is a student who almost never stands up, specifically try to get that person to stand up when "it" by saying something you have in common with the student—for example, "I'm wearing black shoes," or "I have brown eyes."

Selection of Group Name (If Time Allows)

This activity builds group cohesion. The students decide on a name for their group that will be used throughout later groups. Introduce this activity by saying, **"Now we'll need a name for our group. First let's try to come up with as many possible names as we can think of, then we'll vote on the one you all like best."**

1. Group members generate a list of names, which you write down on a large sheet of paper. Accept any name at this stage, no matter how strange or silly. Group names have included "The Trustworthy Club," "Yo Mama," the "UCLA Club," "The Hustlers," and even "Bruins [UCLA team name] and Buttheads." It is the members' group name, and it is up to them to decide on one they like. In some groups, the boys or the girls will take over this activity. Try to help both genders suggest names.

2. Vote on group name. Once students have generated a large list, say, **"OK, now we have a list of names. Everyone can have two votes, so look on the list and decide on the two names you like the best. Now, who votes for [first name on the list]?"** Tally responses. If there is a tie, have students vote between the two remaining names. **"We have a winner. Our group name is [Name of Group]."**

Check-Out

Check-out is a time for students to process their reactions to the group, and to reinforce major points of each lesson. Introduce Check-out by saying, **"Our last activity for every group is called Check-out. This is a time for us to talk about our reactions to the group. What were your reactions to the group today? Was it the same or different from what you expected? What did you notice in the Me Too game? Were there parts of the group you liked or didn't like? Are there things that you would like to do more?"** Go around the circle and ask students to respond.

Note: If the group is very difficult to manage, be prepared to develop group rules. See Session Two for directions.

Session Two

Activities
  ✔ Check-in
  ✔ Introduce new members; discuss confidentiality
  ✔ Group rules
  ✔ Feelings Grab Bag

✔ Group name (if not done in Session One)

✔ Check-out

Materials   ✔ Curriculum

✔ Trust ratings (one copy for each student who was not present at Session One—see Appendix B-1a)

✔ Confidentiality Contracts (one copy for each student who did not sign during Session One—see Appendix B-1b)

✔ A hat or bag for Feelings Grab Bag

✔ Feelings for Feelings Grab Bag (one copy for each group—see Appendix B-1c; cut and fold each feeling)

✔ A pad of paper large enough to be seen by all students

✔ Brightly colored pens for writing on the pad of paper

✔ Masking tape for putting up sheets of poster paper

Content

Check-In

This activity gives students an opportunity to bring up things that are happening in their lives that might need to be discussed in the group. Examples might be a death in the family, a loved one going to jail, or a fight in the school.

Introduce Check-in by saying, "**Each week we will start the group with an activity called Check-in. We would like to go around the circle and have each person say their name and tell the group how things are going for them. The reason we have this activity is to give you a chance to bring up things that you would like to talk about in the group. We have activities planned for each week, but sometimes things happen in people's lives, and we want to be able to have time to talk about those things, too. For example, in other groups we have done, students have had a birthday, have gotten in trouble at school, had a fun party, had family members who have died, gotten a good grade on a test, or have had parents divorce. These are things they have brought up in group. Who wants to start this week?**" Encourage participation from each member.

Introduce Any New Group Members

Use the same procedure as week one. Let other group members relate things like confidentiality, purpose of the group, and activities to help them feel ownership and to make sure they understood. For example, the leader might ask, "**Who can tell James what confidentiality is?**"

1. Give new members Confidentiality Contracts to sign. Make sure all members have signed the contracts by the end of the session.

2. If students feel they cannot sign the Confidentiality Contract, they cannot continue in the group.

Group Rules

The goal is to help group members develop a feeling of group ownership. Group members are called on to generate, set consequences for, and enforce their own rules, rather than being required to follow rules that have been imposed on them. This shifts the role of disciplinarian from the leader to the group members (with the help of reminders from the leader). Setting up rules may need to be done in Session One, depending on the composition of the group. Middle-school groups almost always need group rules by the end of Session Two; for high-school groups, rules are instituted when and if needed.

Generating Rules

Say something like, **"Now we're going to talk about group rules. We already have one rule, confidentiality. We also have some school rules that we need to keep. For example, we need to stay in the room during group rather than wandering around school. However, we don't have any other rules yet. We want this to be a place where you can feel comfortable talking about difficult subjects and can trust the other group members. We value and want to hear about everyone's opinions and feelings, and we want to make this a safe place to talk about them. Because this is your group, you can make the rules. Let's come up with possible rules. Then you can vote on which ones will help you best. Who has an idea for a rule that you think will make this the kind of place where you can talk about things that are important to you?"**

1. Generate a list of rules. Accept any suggestions at this point. Then say, **"OK, now we have a list of possible rules. Remember, the reason for the rules is to make this a place where you will feel safe and comfortable talking about things that are important to you. Let's talk about and vote on which rules will make the group feel safe."**

2. Allow for discussion of and a vote on each rule separately. If a rule is proposed that you perceive will be problematic and students do not first point out the difficulties, you can pose a question to get the group thinking about the possible consequences of the rule—for example, "If we have a rule that people can throw things at other people, I wonder if the group will feel like a safe place."

Generating Consequences

Say something like, **"Now we have some group rules. What are going to be the consequences if a group member breaks a rule?"**

1. Generate a list; discuss the suggestions using a format similar to the one used for generating rules; then vote on the suggestions.

2. This part of the activity requires some careful responding by the group leader. The most useful consequences are something similar to one or two warnings, a time-out (remember to set a length, such as 3 or 5 minutes), then getting sent back to class for the day. Gently guide students toward such consequences.

   a. During the discussion, again ask questions to raise issues that might interfere with the success of the consequence—for example, "How long do you think it would take to write 'I will not bother other group members' 100 times?"

   b. If the group wants to set up other consequences that you think are reasonable, then these will be the consequences (e.g., do 10 push-ups, write a standard 10 times).

3. The goal of a time-out is time away from the attention of the group. When discussing time-outs, discourage attention-seeking time-outs such as "standing in the middle of the circle with a book on your head and your arms in the air."

   a. When in time-out, the student should sit in a chair in a corner of the room, facing away from the group. Do not lecture the student on the way to the chair because the added attention is often reinforcing, but quietly help the student to the time-out chair if necessary.

   b. If the student gets up or is disruptive, the time-out starts over again. Try to keep the group engaging for the other students while the time-out is taking place because you don't want the student in time-out to get attention (though he or she will probably try for attention).

   c. It is important to keep track of the time. When the time-out is over, invite the student to return to the group. Try to help make the student integral to the ongoing activity since the consequence is over and the student is not being punished.

Enforcing Rules and Consequences
It is important to be consistent and careful in enforcing the rules and consequences. There is a temptation to overlook rule violations in early group sessions. Do not give in to this temptation, because then the group does not develop trust in the safety of the group environment. Even if you have to send a student back to class one week, the next week the student usually returns with increased respect for the rules and your ability to ensure the group's safety.

1. Group members are encouraged to be the ones who enforce the rules. If they do not call a rule violation that you see, you can say, **"Does anyone see a rule being broken?"** It is important for group cohesion and self-esteem to allow students to actively and effectively enforce the rules and consequences they have established.

2. After Session Two, use poster board or butcher paper to neatly write up the group rules and consequences. The heading should be the group's name to encourage group cohesion. This paper or board should be hung up in the room for each later session.

Trust Building Activity: Feelings Grab Bag (Adapted from Pedro-Carroll, 1985)

The goal of this activity is to increase awareness of one's own and other's emotions. It gives group members practice in identifying and reflecting feelings, the first building block toward developing empathic ways of responding. It is similar to charades, with the following steps: (1) a student draws a feeling out of the grab bag (a hat or bag); (2) the student acts out the feeling in front of the group, and members try to guess the feeling; (3) once the feeling is guessed, the student tells a time he or she has felt that feeling; (4) everyone else in the group gives an example of a time they felt the identified feeling.

1. Introduce this game by saying, **"Now we are going to play a game to help us learn how to help each other with problems. Have you ever had a friend tell you about a problem? Well, sometimes it's helpful just to let the person know that you understand how they feel by saying something like 'You must be mad' or 'That'd make me so sad.' Sometimes it can be hard to tell how someone else is feeling. So we're going to do this game to help us practice recognizing different feelings in our friends."**

2. **"This game is called Feelings Grab Bag. It's kind of like charades. Has anyone played charades? We have a number of feelings in this hat [or bag]. Each group member is going to get a chance to reach into the grab bag and draw a feeling. Then you'll come up to the front and act out the feeling for the other group members. Everyone tries to guess what the feeling is. Once someone guesses the feeling, the actor tells a time when he or she felt that feeling. Then everyone else in the group tells a time they felt like that. If you get a feeling that is really hard to act out, you can pick someone in the group to help you act out the feeling. OK, who wants to start?"**

3. If there's time after everyone has had a turn, discuss which feelings are the easiest and the hardest to express and why. Remind students that they can help people feel more comfortable talking about problems in the group just by recognizing and naming the other person's feeling.

Selection of Group Name

(If not done in Session One—see Session One for instructions.)

Check-Out

Generally, same as Session One. Ask, **"Why did we do Feelings Grab Bag? What did we learn that will help others when they are hurting?"**

Session Three

Activities
    ✔ Trust ratings

    ✔ Check-in

✔ Secret Pooling

✔ Check-out

Materials
✔ Curriculum

✔ Trust ratings (one copy for each student—see Appendix B-1a)

✔ Confidentiality Contracts (for any student who missed Sessions One and Two—see Appendix B-1b)

✔ Secrets for Low-Trust Secret Pooling activity (see Appendix B-1d)

✔ Helping Responses handout—one copy for each student (see Appendix B-1e)

✔ Paper and pencils for writing secrets in High-Trust version

✔ Hat or bag in which to put secrets

✔ Masking tape

✔ Rules and consequences (if generated in previous session). These should be put up in the room before each group session.

Content

Trust Ratings

Have each group member fill out a trust rating slip. Collect them and put them aside. The level of trust in the group will be used to determine the version of the Secret Pooling activity you use later in this session.

Check-In

See Session Two.

Trust-Building Activity: Secret Pooling (Adapted from Goodman & Esterly, 1988)

This activity allows group members to practice and reinforce the skills in empathic responding taught in the first two sessions. It also reinforces self-disclosure skills when group members hear their secrets being read and hopefully met with empathy and understanding. In addition, hearing secrets that are similar to their own experiences reinforces feelings of universality for group members. This activity has the following steps: (1) a student draws a secret out of a hat or bag; (2) the student reads the secret as if it were his or her own secret; (3) the student says how he or she would feel if the secret were his or hers; (4) other students are encouraged to say how they think the person with that secret would be feeling; (5) group members are encouraged to discuss what they could say or do to help the person with the secret. There are High-Trust and Low-Trust versions of Secret Pooling. Prior to the group session, copy and cut out the prewritten secrets for the Low-Trust version (Appendix B-1d), fold them, and place them in a hat or bag, in case they are needed.

Low-Trust Version of Secret Pooling
The Low-Trust version is used if the trust ratings generated at the beginning of Session Three show an average trust rating of less than 3.

1. Say, "Today we are going to play a game called Secret Pooling. We have a number of secrets written down and placed in this hat [or bag]. We'd like you to draw a secret out of the hat [or bag]. Then please read the secret to yourself and think about how you would feel if it were your secret."

2. "Then when it's your turn, please read the secret out loud as if it were your own secret and say what feelings you'd be having. Other group members can help come up with feelings."

3. "Finally, we'd like the other group members to think about what they could say that would help the person with this secret feel better."

4. "We have a handout that gives ideas on how to be helpful to someone who shares a problem [pass out Helping Responses handout]. As you can see, the two most helpful things are:

   a. "Reflect the person's feeling, so they feel understood.

   b. "Share a time when something similar happened to you and how you felt, so they don't feel so alone."

5. "Make sure to put empathy and helping the other person above curiosity. Ready? OK, who wants to begin?"

High-Trust Version of Secret Pooling
The High-Trust version is used if the trust ratings generated at the beginning of Session Three show an average trust rating of 3 or higher. In this version, students are asked to generate their own secrets.

1. Say, "Today we are going to play a game called Secret Pooling. Before we begin, we will ask each of you to write down a secret about yourself that you think no one in the group will know. For example, people sometimes say something about their families (like if their parents are getting a divorce), about themselves (like if they've been arrested or used drugs), or about their relationships with others (like if they've had sex). Don't put your name on the paper. We don't want anyone to know that the secret is yours. Once we have your secrets, we're going to fold them in half, put them in the hat [or bag] and start the game." Pass out paper and pencils, and ask the students to write down their secrets.

2. "We'd like you to draw a secret out of the hat [or bag]. If you get the secret that you wrote, put it back and draw another secret. Then please read the secret to yourself and think about how you would feel if that were your secret."

3. "Then when it's your turn, please read the secret out loud as if it were your own secret and say what feelings you'd be having. Other group members can help come up with feelings. Now the most important thing here is to talk about the feelings a person with this secret would have."

4. "We do not want you to try to guess whose secret it is or ask other group members if they wrote the secret. Also, do not reveal which secret is yours. And remember our Confidentiality Contract, and do not share anything with people outside the group."

5. "Finally, we'd like the other group members to think about what they could say that would help the person with this secret feel better. We have a handout that gives ideas on how to be helpful to someone who shares a problem [pass out Helping Responses handout]. As you can see, the two most helpful things are:

   a. "Reflect the person's feeling, so they feel understood.

   b. "Share a time when something similar happened to you and how you felt, so they don't feel so alone."

6. "Make sure to put empathy and helping the other person above curiosity. Ready? OK, who wants to begin?"

7. Leaders need to actively discourage members from trying to guess the author of the secret in the High-Trust version. A reminder about confidentiality can be helpful.

Responses to Secret Pooling
In both versions, encourage group members to respond to the secret-teller. The focus is on what will be helpful to the secret-teller. Encourage reflection of feelings. If another student discloses a similar experience, the helpfulness of such self-disclosure to the person with the secret is emphasized.

1. Encouraged responses:

   a. *Reflections:* "That must be so hard for you," "You must feel sad all the time," and so on. If group members do not make feeling reflections, you can model them.

   b. *Self-disclosure:* "I think I know how you feel, because I also got picked up by the police (or had my dad leave without warning, etc.)."

2. Discouraged responses:

   a. *Advice-giving:* If students respond by giving advice, say "**I wonder how _____ feels. It will be more helpful for them to feel understood than be told what to do.**"

   b. *Lots of specific questions about facts* (e.g., "What other drugs have you tried? Did the police pick you up other times too? How many guys have you had sex with?"): Say, "**I wonder how _____ feels. Let's see if we can help [him or her] feel understood.**"

3. Especially when the secrets presented are highly personal (whether their own or given to them), there may be a tendency for students to react with nervous laughter or make jokes. It is important to quickly intervene and ask the group how they would feel if it were their own secret that they finally could share, and people laughed or made fun of it.

4. After all the secrets are presented, hold a general discussion about what feels helpful when you are talking about something that is hard or scary to talk about and what makes you feel vulnerable.

Check-Out

Elicit general reactions to the session. Then ask, **"What did we learn from Secret Pooling? What things seemed to help the person with the secret feel understood? What felt helpful to you when you told the secret?"**

Anger Management and Problem-Solving Skills

Note: This module is extremely important, and may take three sessions if necessary.

Goal To help students learn to generate and practice nonviolent responses when angry or provoked

Overview of Sessions

Session One
- *Purpose:* Overview of basic problem-solving skills, understanding what makes one angry (including internal and external triggers), examining typical responses to anger and generating alternative responses, exploring consequences and pros and cons of violent and nonviolent responses

- *Content:* (1) Problem-Solving cartoon, (2) Anger management: What makes us angry, options for reacting when angry, consequences of the options, (3) Hot-Head Cool-Head card game

Session Two
- *Purpose:* Further examination of alternatives in dealing with anger, practicing Cool-Head responses

- *Content:* Hot-Head Cool-Head role play

Session One

Activities
- ✔ Check-in

- ✔ Problem-Solving cartoon

- ✔ Anger management
  1. What makes us angry?
  2. Options for reacting when angry
  3. Consequences of the options

✔ Hot-Head Cool-Head card game

✔ Check-out and handout

Materials   ✔ Curriculum

✔ Problem-Solving cartoon (one copy for each student—see Appendix B-2a)

✔ Large pad of paper

✔ Colored markers

✔ Masking tape

✔ Hot-Head Cool-Head game cards (see Appendix B-2b)

✔ Cool-Head Responses handout (one copy for each student—see Appendix B-2c)

✔ Rules and consequences with the group name at the top of the rules and consequences pages. Put these up in the room before each session.

Content

Check-In

Problem-Solving Cartoon (Adapted from Pedro-Carroll, 1985)

This activity presents a basic format for dealing with interpersonal problems that includes (1) identifying the problem; (2) generating alternative solutions; (3) examining the consequences of each option; (4) making an informed choice among the options; (5) evaluating the outcome of the decision.

1. Give each student a copy of the Problem-Solving cartoon. Read through the cartoon together, briefly discussing each of the problem-solving steps.

2. Say, **"Today we are going to discuss how we deal with different kinds of problems. We're going to spend the first few minutes reading through this cartoon together, and then move on to talking about how we all deal with different problems, especially anger. Who will read the first box of the cartoon?"**

3. Summarize each of the boxes as they are read, using the language of this module (e.g., Box 1 of the cartoon refers to a "problem"; in Box 2 the boy is considering different "alternatives"; and in Boxes 3 and 6 he is evaluating the "consequences").

4. Begin to focus discussion on anger—for example: **"Dealing with anger and conflict is a big problem for many people. Now we're going to try to use the**

problem-solving steps of the cartoon to help us look at different ways of dealing with anger and resolving conflicts."

Anger Management

In this activity, students are encouraged to examine internal and external triggers to anger; the concepts of hot-headed and cool-headed alternatives are introduced; and the idea of anticipating the consequences of actions is discussed.

What Makes Us Angry?

Referring to the Problem-Solving cartoon, say, **"What is the problem? What are some of the things that make us angry?"** Have the group generate a list of things or situations that make them angry. Write down responses on the left side of the large pad of paper, helping members generate a representative list of anger-provoking situations.

1. If the group does not spontaneously produce them, suggest some internal triggers (e.g., perceptions—"Sometimes we say things to ourselves, like 'He's trying to make me look like a punk,' that make us feel even more angry . . .").

2. Have group members discuss how they know they're angry (i.e., physiological triggers, such as racing heart, clenched fists, hot face).

Alternatives for Reacting When Angry

Referring to the Problem-Solving cartoon, say, **"What are some of our options when we are angry?"**

1. Introduce idea of hot-headed and cool-headed responses. Say, **"Most ways we deal with anger fall into two categories, and we're going to call those categories hot-headed and cool-headed responses. What do you think might be some hot-headed ways of dealing with anger? What might be some cool-headed ways of dealing with anger?"** If the group has trouble coming up with cool-headed responses, suggest some, such as walking away or self-instruction ("Just relax" or "Maybe she didn't mean to bump me").

2. On the right side of the previously generated list of anger-provoking situations, ask students how they would react to these situations. Then ask if each response is a hot-headed or a cool-headed response. Encourage students to generate a hot-headed and a cool-headed response for each situation.

3. Point out that not expressing anger in some form may have negative consequences as well (e.g., exploding later on or taking out one's anger on an innocent victim).

4. If students simply cannot relate to cool-headed responses because they feel such responses would be too wimpy, you can raise the possibility of using "warm-headed" responses. Warm-headed responses involve giving back a verbal insult, making fun of the insult itself (e.g., "That line's so old you must have learned it from your great-grandmother"), or threatening to come back later. The possibil-

ity of warm-headed responses should be raised only after working to help students feel comfortable with cool-headed responses.

Consequences of the Alternatives

Referring to the Problem-Solving cartoon, say, **"What are some of the consequences of each of these alternatives?"**

1. Introduce concepts of (a) short-term versus long-term consequences, and (b) consequences for oneself versus others. Say, **"What are some of the things that might happen if we choose these different alternatives? For most of them, there would probably be some good things that might come out of it and some bad things. Also, the consequences might change over time. There might be a good consequence over the short-term, for example, but a bad consequence over the long-term. Also, the consequences might be good for some people and bad for other people."**

2. Using as examples a few of the anger-provoking situations and alternatives previously generated, ask students to discuss the consequences of the alternatives, focusing on short-term versus long-term consequences and consequences for self versus others. For example, **"So what would happen if you hit him after he called you a sissy? What would be the consequence for him and for you right after? What might happen later on?"** It is important to recognize that the short-term consequence of a hot-headed response might feel positive for the student, in that he or she would feel powerful and vindicated and friends would look up to him or her. However, the long-term consequence might be suspension from school for fighting or retaliation by rival gang members.

Anger Management Activity: Hot-Head Cool-Head Card Game

(Start this activity if time permits. If not, do it next week.) This activity reinforces the concepts of identifying an anger-provoking situation, choosing cool-headed or hot-headed alternatives, and evaluating the consequences of the chosen alternative.

1. Set up the three stacks of cards, Problem, Alternative, and Consequence. Either use the preprinted problem cards from Appendix B-2b, or write out your own problem cards to fit the needs of the group.

2. The first player selects a Problem card and reads the problem aloud to the group.

3. The person to the left then selects an Alternative card, which will read either "hot" or "cool"; the player must provide an appropriate hot-headed or cool-headed response.

4. The next person to the left then draws a Consequence card (e.g., "Long-term for the other person") and must provide an appropriate consequence for the response just described.

Check-Out

Elicit general reactions from the group. Especially if there was not time for the card game, this session may be viewed as boring. In this case, let members know that next time they'll use what they learned to play a really cool game. Ask, **"What are some things we learned about dealing with anger today? Why should we look at different alternatives? Why is it important to look at possible consequences?"** Give each member a copy of the Cool-Head Response handout, saying, **"I'd like you all to do an experiment this week. Use two cool-headed responses this week, and tell us how it went next week."**

Session Two

Activities
- ✔ Check-in
- ✔ Go over Cool-Head Responses handout
- ✔ Review Problem-Solving cartoon
- ✔ Hot-Head Cool-Head card game (if not played last session)
- ✔ Hot-Head Cool-Head role play
- ✔ Check-out

Materials
- ✔ Curriculum
- ✔ Problem-Solving cartoon (see Appendix B-2a)
- ✔ Hot-Head Cool-Head card game (if not played last session—see Appendix B-2b)
- ✔ Rules and consequences with the group name at the top of the rules and consequences pages. Put these up in the room before each session.

Content

Check-In

Review of Cool-Head Responses Handout

Go over the handout and check on students' use of cool-headed responses during the last week. If a student chose a hot-headed response during the week, work with the group to generate a cool-headed response that the student would feel comfortable using in a similar situation.

Review of Problem-Solving Cartoon

Remind participants to look at alternatives and consequences.

Hot-Head Cool-Head Card Game

(If not played last session. See last session's curriculum for a description.)

Anger Management Activity: Hot-Head Cool-Head Role Play

The goal is to actively involve the students in evaluating cool-headed and hot-headed responses in simulated situations. Besides providing a review of problem-solving skills, the activity gives some understanding of how to resolve, or at least how not to exacerbate, conflicts between others. The activity has the following steps: (1) Group members are divided into two groups (with at least four members in each group), and each group does a role play. (2) In the role play, the "good guy" and "bad guy" get into an argument, then "freeze." (3) While they are frozen, the other two actors advise the good guy. The "hot-head" tries to get the good guy to respond violently. The "cool-head" tries to get the good guy to respond nonviolently. (4) The good guy chooses which response to use, and tells why that response was chosen. (5) Each group does their role play while the other group watches.

1. Introduce the activity by saying, **"Has anyone ever seen those cartoons where the character has an angel on one shoulder and a devil on the other, and they're both trying to get him to do different things?"** Process reactions. **"Well, today's activity is kind of like that. We are going to break into two teams, and each team is going to put on a short play for the other team. OK, let's break into teams."** (You can assign teams or let group members choose.)

2. Say, **"Remember last time when we asked you about situations that make people angry? The play is going to be about those situations. Each team needs to pick one situation. Then each team picks who will play the characters. Each team's play should have a 'good guy,' a 'bad guy,' a 'cool-head,' and a 'hot-head'."**

   a. **"The role of the cool-head is to serve as a kind of good 'conscience' and advise the good guy on ways to avoid violence. The cool-head character may suggest some of the 'cooling off' techniques we talked about."**

   b. **"The hot-head character may represent the good guy's automatic response or pressures to 'save face' and respond with violence. The hot-head character is to act like a 'bad conscience.'"**

   c. **"The purpose of the role play is for the good guy to examine the consequences of both the 'hot-head' and 'cool-head' responses. Then the good guy will tell us what he or she chooses and why."**

3. **"This is how it will work. The bad guy will start provoking and trying to get the good guy mad. When I say 'freeze,' the hot-head and the cool-head will each try to influence the good guy to follow them. After they finish, then the good guy will make the choice. Then you will do your play for the other group."**

4. You should assist in the development of the role plays in order to ensure that the participants understand the purpose of the activity. Help assign characters in ways that will be productive: For example, it is best to avoid having a shy child play the cool-head role; if possible, the cool-head role should be performed by a

student with high status in the group. It is helpful for you to facilitate the choice of a cool-headed response by asking questions about the consequences of a hot-headed response.

5. Once each group has planned the role play, they perform for the other group. Encourage good audience behavior from the group not performing (i.e., paying attention, not shouting out, etc.). The good guy and bad guy begin to argue; when it escalates, say **"freeze,"** and the actors stop moving. Then the hot-head and cool-head try to convince the good guy of his next action.

6. If the role plays are not resolved in nonviolent ways, generate group discussion as to why. Sometimes students focus on the immediate consequence of winning or showing off and do not examine the longer-term consequences. Work with members to generate an alternative cool-headed response that they find acceptable.

Check-Out

Elicit general reactions from the students. Then ask, **"What did we learn and practice today about dealing with situations that make us angry?"** If the students' responses do not mention cool-headed and hot-headed responses, looking at alternatives, and evaluating the consequences, reiterate these points.

Ethnic Identity and Anti-Prejudice

Goal To help students develop positive feelings of ethnic pride, to address and discuss prejudice, and to understand and accept people from other ethnic groups

Overview of Sessions

Session One
- *Purpose:* To increase awareness and understanding of prejudice and stereotypes
- *Content:* (1) Labeling game, (2) discussion of stereotypes and prejudice

Session Two
- *Purpose:* To help students examine societal examples of racism, further understand how racism influences behavior, and make a commitment to eliminating racism
- *Content:* (1) "True Colors" video episode of *PrimeTime Live*—other video material portraying blatant racism can be substituted, (2) what can we do about discrimination and prejudice?

Session Three
- *Purpose:* To continue discussion of prejudice, and to discuss and strengthen one's own ethnic identity
- *Content:* Ethnic identity posters

Session One

Activities
- ✔ Check-in
- ✔ Labeling game
- ✔ Discussion of stereotypes and prejudice
- ✔ Check-out

Materials

✔ Curriculum

✔ Name tag labels with adjectives written on them for labeling exercise (see Appendix B-3)

✔ Masking tape

✔ Rules and consequences with the group name at the top of the rules and consequences pages. Put these up in the room before each session.

Content

Check-In

Anti-Prejudice Activity: Labeling Game

The goal is to increase awareness and understanding of prejudice and stereotypes. This game has the following steps: (1) Place a label on each group member's forehead; (2) group members mingle, treating each other as if the labels were true; (3) group members try to guess their label based on the way they were treated.

1. Before the group meets, prepare adhesive labels (mailing labels or name tag stickers) with adjectives or descriptions written on them. Some should be positive (e.g., Friendly, Helpful, Sexy, Good Athlete, Good Student) and others should be slightly negative (e.g., Snobby, Teacher's Pet, Bossy, Lazy, Shy). Suggested adjectives are given in Appendix B-3. Use the ones most appropriate for your group or those that will be most helpful to your group.

2. Introduce the activity by saying, **"Now we are going to play a game called Labeling. I am going to place a label on each person's forehead so that no one can see his or her own label. Then we will mingle and chat with each other, and you should treat each person as if his or her label is true. For example, if my label said Leader, you might want to ask my advice or follow my lead. The object of the game is to try to guess your label based on how others treat you. There are only three rules:**

   a. **"You can't look at your own label.**

   b. **"You can't tell anyone what their label says.**

   c. **"You can't ask other people to tell you what your label says.**

   "OK. Let's start."

3. Place the labels on students' foreheads. Model the interactions by treating group members stereotypically as if their label were true. Make sure to interact with any students who may not be actively participating.

4. After 5 or 10 minutes of interacting, ask group members to guess what their labels say. Then have them take off their labels and see what they say.

   a. Encourage students to explain how they guessed their labels from clues from other students by asking, **"How could you tell?"**

   b. Probe how it felt to be treated as if the label were true by asking: **"How did it feel to be treated as if you were _____ ?"**

Discussion of Prejudice and Stereotypes

Say, **"We all wear labels, and people treat us as if the labels were true. Many people look at us and make assumptions. Race or ethnicity is one characteristic that often leads people to make assumptions about others."**

Defining Race and Culture
"Who knows what 'race' means?" Elicit and discuss responses from group members. **"Who knows what 'culture' means? How is it different from 'race'?"** Elicit and discuss responses from group members. **"Sometimes people don't like to talk about race because it makes them feel uncomfortable and makes us seem different from each other. People *are* different, and there's nothing wrong with that. In fact, differences make life interesting. Our race and cultural backgrounds are real and important parts of us, and there is nothing wrong with talking about them. It can help us understand ourselves and others better."**

Defining and Discussing Prejudice
"Who can tell me what 'prejudice' means?" (Support all answers, working toward correct definition.) Prejudice—to prejudge; a feeling, opinion, or attitude about members of a certain group.

1. Ask, **"What's the name for prejudice against**

   a. **people from other racial groups?"** Racism.

   b. **women?"** Sexism.

   c. **people with little money or poor people?"** Classism.

2. It helps group members open up to group leaders of different ethnic backgrounds if you say something like, **"I really hope that you will feel comfortable talking about prejudice with me. I will not feel any differently about you or be mad at you if you say something negative about [leader's ethnicity] people. What's most important to me is to hear your true reactions and feelings about things."**

Defining and Discussing Stereotypes
"Prejudice is often based on stereotypes. Who can tell me what 'stereotype' means?" Stereotypes—exaggerated beliefs about characteristics of members of certain groups, (e.g., Asians are good in math and very quiet; African Americans are violent and good at basketball).

1. Ask, "**What are some examples of stereotypes you've heard, either about your own group or others?**"

2. Elicit examples of people who do not fit these stereotypes.

Exploration of Origins of Prejudice

Say, "**It is probably impossible to grow up without any prejudice because it is such a problem in our society and is very common.**"

1. Examine origins of our racial attitudes. "**Where do these attitudes come from? Where did you learn some of the stereotypes you have?**" Common sources are parents, media, and school.

2. The following are suggested questions for discussion.

   a. Describe the earliest memory you have of an experience with people of a cultural or ethnic group different from yours.

   b. Who or what has had the most influence on how you feel about people of different cultural or racial groups, and in what ways?

   c. What changes, if any, would you like to make in your own attitudes or experiences in relation to people of other ethnic groups?

   d. Describe an experience where you feel you were discriminated against for any reason, not necessarily race or culture. (Point out that all people experience some kind of prejudice, maybe because of race, gender, class, religion, style of dress, but acknowledge that some groups experience more prejudice than others.)

3. If members have trouble talking about experiences of prejudice, share a personal experience of prejudice, including feelings and coping style.

Check-Out

Elicit general responses about the session. Then ask, "**What was the point of the labeling game? What did we learn about prejudice and stereotypes?**"

Note: **Begin to plan for the field trip now. See Module Four, Session Two for details on how to plan the field trip.**

Session Two

Activities

✔ Check-in

✔ Watch "True Colors" video (or other video showing clear-cut racial discrimination)

✔ What can we do about discrimination and prejudice?

✔ Check-out

Materials   ✔ Curriculum

✔ "True Colors" episode of *PrimeTime Live* videotape available through Core Vision Media, 1359 Barclay Blvd., Buffalo Grove, IL 60089, (800) 537-3130, or other video showing clear-cut racial discrimination. Teaching Tolerance has a video called "The Shadow of Hate" (available through the Southern Poverty Law Center, 400 Washington Ave., P.O. Box 548, Montgomery, AL 36101-0548).

✔ TV and VCR

✔ Masking tape

✔ Rules and consequences with the group name at the top of the rules and consequences pages. Put these up in the room before each session.

Content

Check-In

Discrimination in Society: "True Colors" Episode of PrimeTime Live *(or other video showing clear-cut racial discrimination)*

The goal is to graphically display instances of societal racism. Before beginning the video, say, **"Today we're going to talk more about prejudice. We're going to watch a TV show. This show usually brings out a lot of feelings in people. Some people feel angry when they watch this, others feel sad or confused. After we watch this, we'll talk about the kinds of feelings it brings up for us."**

Show Video
The "True Colors" video shows two men, one African American and the other white, doing the same activities (e.g., applying for a job, renting an apartment, buying a car) and being treated very differently. As previously mentioned, other video clips showing clear-cut discrimination can be substituted.

Discuss the Film
There may be many strong responses, especially among older students. Sometimes young middle-school students have trouble relating to the video. Encourage students to express their feelings (e.g., anger, sadness, fearfulness, helplessness).

1. Ask, **"Have any of you had experiences like those in the film? Have you ever been treated differently because of your race or ethnicity?"** Share your reactions to model that having feelings of anger about injustice can be appropriate.

2. If there have been recent publicized instances of discrimination in your community, bring them up and elicit reactions from the students.

What Can We Do about Discrimination and Prejudice?

(If time allows. If the discussion does not wind down, this section should begin Session Three of this module.) The goal is for students to make a commitment to do their part to eliminate racism. If appropriate, say, **"It sounds like many of you have had experiences with racism and that prejudice seems unfair and hurtful. Several of you raised the question 'What can we do about this?'"** (If no one raised that question, say, **"Let's talk about what we can do to stop prejudice."**)

1. Explore students' own stereotypes. **"One of the biggest ways we can make a difference is by changing our own behaviors. Because of the way our society is, most people hold stereotypes and have acted in a way that was prejudiced. Who can tell us about a stereotype they've held or something they've done or said that you think might have been kind of prejudiced?"**

    a. Reinforce being brave enough to speak up. Encourage others to share their attitudes and experiences.

    b. In schools with much racial tension, this may be a difficult and emotionally charged activity. Acknowledge that by saying, **"We know that discrimination and prejudice occur right here in our school, so it's kind of a touchy subject. But it's important to own up to what's happening so that we can do something about it. Who can give some examples of discrimination or prejudice going on at our school?"**

2. Generate ideas about things group members can do to lessen racism. Say, **"Who has ideas about what *we* can do to eliminate racism?"** If students are unable to come up with ideas, suggest some of the following (or your own ideas): not laughing at racist jokes, asking friends and relatives not to tell racist jokes or make prejudiced statements, talking in a friendly manner with members of other ethnic groups.

Check-Out

Elicit general reactions to the session. If very strong feelings were aroused, be sure to validate them. **"Yes, the video made many of us very upset and angry."** Ask, **"What positive steps can we take to deal with the feelings we had about the discrimination we saw on the video?"**

Session Three

Activities   ✔ Check-in

✔ Finish "What can we do about discrimination and prejudice?" if not completed last session

✔ Ethnic Identity posters

✔ Check-out

Materials   ✔ Curriculum

✔ Poster boards (at least enough for each ethnic group represented)

✔ Colored markers (lots)

✔ Permission slips for field trip to local university or college

✔ Masking tape

✔ Rules and consequences with the group name at the top of the rules and the consequences pages. Put these up in the room before each session.

Content

Check-In

What Can We Do about Discrimination and Prejudice?

If the discussion from Session Two feels unfinished, say, "**Last week we watched a video where an African American man and a Caucasian man tried to get a job, rent an apartment, and buy a car. They were treated very differently.** [Modify the above as necessary to fit the details of the video shown in Session Two.] **We started talking about people's experiences with racism and some of the anger and fear that people feel when they are discriminated against. I'm wondering if you have thought any more about this during the week.**" Process responses according to the guidelines in Session Two.

Ethnic Pride Activity: Ethnic Identity Posters

(Requires at least one-half hour.) The goal is to develop and share a sense of ethnic identity and to celebrate differences and diversity. This activity has the following steps: (1) Members break up into small groups of the same ethnicity; (2) groups share ideas and feelings about what it means to be a member of that ethnic group; (3) group members draw symbols representing these ideas and feelings on posters; (4) the groups come together and present their posters to each other; (5) students identify differences and similarities among posters.

1. Students break into groups by ethnicity. If, for example, all students are Latino, then the groups are broken down by country of origin (e.g., Mexico, Puerto Rico, El Salvador).

   a. Say, "**One way that we can feel better when other people treat us in a prejudiced way is to remember the things we like about our own ethnic groups. Today we are going to think about what we especially like about our ethnic groups by making Ethnic Identity posters. We'll make one poster for each ethnic group here. Let's make this area the African American poster, this one the Latino poster, and this one . . .**"

b. **"First discuss your ideas about what it means to be a member of your group and what symbols or concepts or feelings represent your cultural or racial identity. After you have come to an agreement, draw those things on your poster."**

c. If students have trouble thinking about symbols or ideas, suggest foods, music, dress, history, and so on as possible things to think about. Circulate and assist any groups that may be having trouble.

2. Come together again after 15 to 20 minutes. Discuss feelings about the activity. Ask questions such as the following to stimulate discussion:

a. **"How did it feel to separate into small groups of the same race or ethnicity? (Uncomfortable, similar to how it usually is at school, more comfortable talking about your racial identity with people from your ethnic group?)"**

b. **"How did it feel to come back into one group?"**

c. **"How did the size (relative largeness or smallness) of your group make you feel? Did size affect your discussion or your poster? How might the size of a group affect ethnic identity?"**

3. Present the posters. Each group presents its poster, explaining the meanings of the symbols and objects. Possible discussion questions are

a. **"What were the similarities among posters? What were the differences?"**

b. **"Were there differences and/or disagreements within your group about what ethnicity meant to people? How did it feel to have a different idea about your culture than others in your group?"** Note that "There are many differences among individuals within racial groups, and there are many commonalities among ethnic groups."

c. **"What experiences have led to the development of positive feelings about your cultural heritage and background?"**

d. **"What experiences have led to the development of negative feelings, if any, about your cultural heritage and background?"**

Check-Out

Elicit general reactions to the group. Ask, **"What did we learn about ethnic identity? How does ethnic identity relate to prejudice?"** Pass out permission slips for the field trip to the local college or university to be held in a few weeks, specifying where the students should return the permission slips.

Educational Aspirations

Goal To help students set high educational aspirations, to address barriers to academic success, and to identify specific steps students can take to do better in school

Overview of Sessions

Session One
- *Purpose:* To think about educational and career aspirations, discuss steps required to reach goals, and examine barriers to reaching these goals

- *Content:* (1) Peer introduction of career goals, (2) Education and Career Ladder, (3) barriers to education

Session Two
- *Purpose:* To give students the experience of being on a college campus and to expose students to positive role models

- *Content:* Field trip to local college or university

Session Three
- *Purpose:* To associate positive feelings with being a good student and help students define behaviors and skills necessary to do well in school

- *Content:* (1) Good student guided imagery; (2) goal setting

Session One

Activities
- ✔ Check-in
- ✔ Peer introduction of career goals
- ✔ Education and Career Ladder
- ✔ Barriers to education

✔ Goal setting

✔ Check-out

Materials   ✔ Curriculum

✔ Education and Career Ladder (one for each student—see Appendix B-4a)

✔ My Goals sheets (one for each student—see Appendix B-4b)

✔ A pad of paper large enough to be seen by all students (with questions sheet and blank Education Ladder completed *prior* to session—see below)

✔ Real or pretend microphone (optional)

✔ Brightly colored pens

✔ Masking tape

✔ Rules and consequences with the group name at the top of the rules and consequence pages. Put these up in the room before each session.

Content

Check-In

Peer Introduction of Career Goals

The goal is to help students think about what type of career or work they want for themselves in the future. Students are asked to interview their partner in front of the group.

1. Say, **"Today we will be talking about what you want to do when you have finished high school, and how you can reach that goal. You are going to be reporters and interview each other about your future goals. Then we'll come back together, and you will use our reporter's microphone to interview your partner so that the whole group knows about their goals. Each person in the pair will take a turn being the reporter and the person interviewed."**

2. Have students divide into pairs. Assign pairs, or have students pick partners.

3. Say **"Ask your partner the following questions"** [questions should be written on the large pad of paper as well so students can refer to them]:

   a. **"What is your name? (if you don't already know)"**

   b. **"What do you want to do when you grow up?"**

c. "What is your back-up career plan?"

d. "What education or training do you need to become what you want to be? What do you need for your back-up plan?"

4. Allow 5 to 10 minutes for students to interview each other and find out the answers to the above questions. After about 5 minutes, suggest that students switch roles once they have answered the questions, so that the reporter becomes the interviewee and vice versa.

a. Circulate and help students who may need assistance in coming up with their career plan and their back-up career plan, as well as those who may be shy and have difficulty sharing.

b. If there is an odd number of students, pair yourself with one student; the student should interview you, and you should interview the student.

5. After the interviews, gather in a circle again, and say (using real or imaginary microphone), **"We will now present interviews of group members about what they want to do for a job or career, their back-up plans, and how they will get there. Who will be the first reporter?"** (Give real or imaginary microphone to the reporter.) Each student then interviews the partner about career goals and the steps needed to reach the goal. If an answer is left out, ask the reporter, for example, **"So what kind of education or training will Bryan need to be a fireman [lawyer, NBA player, etc.]?"**

6. Accept all career goals. However, if the goal is something illegal (e.g., pimp), gently question whether this is a reasonable goal.

Educational Aspirations Activity: Education and Career Ladder

The goal is to provide students with a picture of the educational or training steps that they need to take in order to reach their career objectives. Before the beginning of the session, use the Education and Career Ladder handout as a guide to write the steps on one of the large sheets of paper. Make a straight line on the left for age and years in school. Make sure to include spaces for preschool, elementary school, middle school, high school, college/university/vocational school, and graduate/professional school. The ladder (with no steps filled in) should be made before the start of the session. Give each student an Educational and Career Ladder handout.

1. Ask, **"What educational steps have you already taken?"**

a. Start with preschool and elementary school so that students feel they have already accomplished some of the steps.

b. As students mention different steps, fill them in on the Education and Career Ladder. Make sure to go in order up the Education and Career Ladder.

2. After high school is on the board, ask students what comes next, making clear that the next steps will differ depending on their career goals.

   a. Using each student's previously given career goal, ask each student. **"What kind of education or training after high school do you need to become a ____ ?"**

   b. If the student does not know, ask other group members. If that still does not elicit the appropriate answer, supply the answer. If you do not know, brainstorm with the group about how the student might find out what is needed to reach the particular career goal.

      (1) Examples of resources are the school's career guidance counselor, professional organizations (e.g., the Plumber's Association), the Internet.

      (2) You can volunteer to find out for the student if it feels as if the task would be overwhelming to the student.

      (3) Be sure to discuss educational or training steps needed for the back-up career goal as well as the main career goal.

   c. Remind students that each step prepares them for the next one, and that they need to try their best at each level because reaching the next level depends on how they do on the previous level. It will not work to begin trying after they finish high school.

   d. If students are interested, share information about your own education.

3. Ask students to write on their Education and Career Ladder handout the specific steps past high school necessary to reach their particular goal. Say **"On your own handout, please write down your career goal and the education or training steps we just talked about that you need to reach your goal. Then you can keep it at home or in your notebook or locker to remind you."**

Barriers to Education

Say, **"Many of you have goals that would require you to go to college. What are some things that might stop you from going to college?"** Elicit their concerns and worries, and discuss them. Speakers at the field trip will also address some of these issues. The following concerns are common (possible student and leader responses are in parentheses):

1. *Financial.* (Scholarships are available; community/junior colleges.)

2. *Social.* ("People in college will be different from me, I'd feel scared to be away from my friends"—but there are usually people from all backgrounds in college; ethnic studies or other organizations exist to help students feel more supported.)

3. *Deserting my community.* (Many low-income students may feel that they are selling out or that they think they are better than others from their communities. Some students may have been told this by peers or family. It is important to acknowledge this, but to point out ways that education can be used to help one's

community. Education does not have to change you in ways you don't want to be changed.)

4. *Deserting my family.* (In some cultures, there may be a lot of pressure to stay in the neighborhood or live at home. Parents very often have not attended college. They may be ambivalent about having the student go to college; while they are excited for the student, they may also have concerns that their children will leave them or become different from them. It is important to be sensitive to what the child wants and to his or her culture. If the student wants to go away to college, discuss concerns about the family and the student's own need for autonomy. If the student feels more comfortable staying near family, explore nearby colleges where the student could visit often or live at home.)

Goal Setting

The goal is to help students translate their long-term career goals into short-term goals that will help them do better in school now. Say, "**I'm passing out a goal sheet to all of you. In order to reach the top of your Education and Career Ladder, you need to do well in school. Please take this sheet home, fill it out, and bring it back when we meet after the field trip. There will be a reward for students who bring back their sheets filled out** [specify reward—usually candy or stickers, but feel free to be ingenious]. **You will write down goals for this school year and what you can do to achieve these goals."**

1. Elicit one or two students' goals and what is needed to achieve them to make sure students understand the assignment.

2. Examples of useful goals are to get better grades, not fail any classes, not get suspended or sent to the principal.

3. Examples of what the student can do to achieve the goals are to do homework, study for tests, pay attention in class instead of talking to friends, not get into fights, not talk back to the teacher.

Check-Out

Elicit general reactions. Ask "**Why is it important to think about how you might reach your career goals now?**" Remind students to return their signed parent permission slips for the field trip and to bring a lunch or money to buy lunch next week for the field trip.

Session Two: Field Trip to Local College or University

Activities   ✔ Travel on bus

✔ Academic demonstration

✔ Inspirational speakers and snack

✔ Visit dorms, gyms, and Student Union

✔ Lunch

✔ Meet athletes (both genders) or enjoy entertainment (often provided by ethnic studies centers)

✔ Group discussion and Check-out

✔ Return to school on bus

Materials   ✔ Curriculum

✔ Parent permission slips

✔ Snack foods and drinks

✔ Extra My Goals sheets (see Appendix B-4b)

✔ Money to loan students for lunch (optional)

✔ Camera and film to take pictures of the students at various locations (optional)

Notes about the Field Trip

1. The goals of the field trip are to expose students to college and make it real for them; to give them the experience of feeling comfortable and welcome on a college campus; and to provide students with role models with whom they can identify.

2. Planning for the field trip must begin at least a month prior to the selected date; sometimes arranging for a bus must be done even earlier.

3. In choosing a site, we suggest picking a public college or university that has high status in the community. However, if such a site is not convenient or available, utilize the college or university that is available.

4. If several groups are running at a school or several schools in a district are participating in the program, all groups can arrange to go on the field trip the same day. If necessary, modules can be switched around so that the Educational Aspirations module comes at the time of the field trip. However, the field trip should not occur until after the Trust Building and Communication Skills module has been completed.

5. The order of activities and the specific activities are suggestions only; details will depend on the availability of resources at the particular college or university. If you cannot arrange all the suggested activities, do your best. It may take a great deal of effort to set up the field trip the first time, but once it has been arranged, coming back for future field trips is relatively simple.

Content

Travel to College or University on Bus

Parent Permission Slips

1. These should be passed out at least 2 weeks prior to the field trip so that you have at least one session to remind students to get the permission slips signed and returned.

2. Permission slips should be turned in to the group leader or the counseling office several days before the trip so that students without permission slips can be tracked down.

Discussion on Bus

1. Share the day's schedule with students.

2. Emphasize when the bus must leave to return to school.

3. Guidelines for the visit on the college campus.

    a. Stay with the group at all times.

    b. The group rules apply on the field trip.

    c. Listen to and be polite to speakers and guides.

    d. Set up a lunch meeting place and time in case anyone gets lost.

4. Elicit and answer student questions.

Academic Demonstration

1. Most colleges and universities have interesting and absorbing demonstrations for prospective students that can be accessed through the admissions office, the ethnic studies centers, or the public information office. It is worth making several phone calls to access such a demonstration because the instructors are used to making presentations to secondary-school students and almost always put on an interesting show.

2. Examples are physics or chemistry demonstrations or a planetarium.

3. If no demonstration is available, arrangements can be made for students to sit in on the class of an interesting and entertaining professor. Do not expect to drop in on a class at random; doing so may be boring and counterproductive, and professors often are not open to having a group of potentially disruptive visitors unless previously arranged.

Inspirational Speakers and Snack

1. Can be done inside or outside.

2. Snack

   a. If resources are available, it is helpful to provide a mid-morning snack (generally chips or cookies and soda). If resources are not available, ask students to bring a snack from home.

   b. Having the snack also helps students pay attention to the inspirational speakers.

3. Aim for two inspirational speakers, one of each of the following types:

   a. Minority or low-income students who have overcome adversities to attend college and are doing well.

      (1) These speakers can usually be found through ethnic studies centers or the admissions outreach office.

      (2) They tell their own inspirational stories.

   b. Financial aid officers.

      (1) They discuss ways in which students from families with few or no financial resources can receive funding that allows them to attend the college or university.

      (2) They often have pads or pencils or even T-shirts that they may give to students as souvenirs—be sure to ask if they have any material or souvenirs to share with the students when you arrange for them to speak.

4. Suggest that each speak for 10 to 15 minutes.

5. Introduce the speakers. Say, **"We have arranged for two people to speak to you about how college can be a reality for each of you. One is a student who comes from a neighborhood like yours, and the other is the person who helps students who think they cannot afford to go to college get the money to be able to study here. Please listen carefully, and then you can ask any questions you have."**

Visit Dorms, Gyms, and Student Union

1. After listening to the speakers, this is a good time for students to tour the fun places of college. If you are familiar with the campus, you can lead an informal tour. If not, or if you would prefer not to lead the tour, college students who give tours for prospective students can give the tour (requires prearrangement, usually through the Admissions Office).

2. *Dorms.* It is helpful and interesting for students to tour the dorms, see what a student room looks like, explore the recreational facilities, and see where college students eat.

3. *Gyms or other recreational areas* (e.g., swimming pool, fitness center). If the campus has a sports stadium that students might have seen on TV, they enjoy visiting it. The fitness center is also often a big draw. Be sure to ask as you enter

whether it is OK for students to use equipment such as treadmills or weights, and let the students know before they begin exploring.

4. *Student Union.* This should be the last stop before lunch. Allow students to wander around the student store, check out various eating facilities, and so on. Many Student Unions have arcades, which are a huge draw for middle-school and high-school students. If you allow students to play in the arcade, set a clear time limit, and make sure they put their lunch money in a safe and separate place before playing.

Lunch

There are three options for lunch: (1) Students bring their lunches; (2) students buy their lunches at campus eateries; (3) lunch is provided for students. Sometimes, a campus group will be willing to donate lunch (e.g., pizzas or sandwiches and soda). This is worth inquiring about when setting up the trip. If lunch is not provided, encourage students to bring a sack lunch. However, if they wish, they can bring money to buy food on campus. If the last stop on the campus tour is the Student Union, they can buy lunch there. Prearrange where students will eat lunch, depending on what or who the entertainment or speakers will be. Usually the speakers or entertainment will suggest a particular location—either indoors or outdoors.

Athlete Speakers and/or Entertainment

1. *Athlete speakers.* If available, athletes whose names or feats are known to the group members are highly valued. Arrangements can be made through the Athletic Department or sometimes through the Admissions Outreach office. The sports figures who choose to speak to students generally speak of their own struggles to go to college and talk about the importance of studying and getting good grades in order to be able to play sports in college. They often bring photos they have signed or that they will personally autograph, providing a very special souvenir. The ideal situation is to have both a male and a female athlete.

2. *Entertainment.* This can usually be arranged through the ethnic studies centers and can take the form of a step or salsa dance demonstration, singers, and so on.

3. If you have to choose between athlete speakers and entertainment, athletes who are known are usually more highly valued by group members. However, whatever can be arranged, either athlete speakers, entertainment, or both, is fine.

Group Discussion and Check-Out

1. After lunch and the speakers or entertainment, find a quiet place where the group can sit in a circle (on grass or at a round table in the Student Union if the weather is poor).

2. Ask, **"So what are some of your impressions from our visit today?"** Guide the discussion with such questions as:

   a. **"Do you think you would like to go to a college like this? Why?"**

b. **"What are some things you especially liked today?"** Students are often impressed that there are no bells and that you do not *have* to go to class. They also may be very taken with the sports figures, the tour guides, "the cute guys," or "the sexy girls."

c. **"Were there any scary parts or things that made you uncomfortable?"** Sometimes students worry about the size of the campus, getting lost, not knowing anyone, or being away from home. If they say they think they could never go to college, then elicit what they see as obstacles, and make sure to include the obstacles in the discussion during the next session.

d. **"Are there other questions you have?"**

e. Say, **"Remember to bring in your goal sheets next week, and we'll talk about what you need to do to reach your goal for this year and for your future."**

Board Buses for Return to School

Session Three

Activities
- ✔ Check-in
- ✔ Guided imagery
- ✔ Discussion of being a good student
- ✔ Discussion of goals
- ✔ Check-out

Materials
- ✔ Curriculum
- ✔ Extra My Goals sheets (see Appendix B-4b)
- ✔ Candy, stickers, or other rewards for students who brought back their My Goals sheets
- ✔ Large pad of paper
- ✔ Markers
- ✔ Masking tape
- ✔ Rules and consequences with the group name at the top of the rules and consequences pages. Put these up in the room before each session.

Content

Check-In

Educational Aspirations Activity: Guided Imagery (Adapted from Campbell, 1991)

The goal is to associate positive feelings with being a good student, discuss rationales for being a good student, and validate and encourage high educational and career aspirations.

1. Say, "Today we are going to do an activity called a 'guided imagery.' So spread out, turn your back to the middle of the circle, and relax. For guided imagery, you will need to use your imagination. Close your eyes, and get in a comfortable position. Put your hands and feet where they are the most comfortable and relaxed. As I talk to you, imagine that with every breath you are becoming more and more relaxed. Now rest your head, take a deep breath [pause], and hear my words. Listen to my voice, and let all the other noises around you fade away. Imagine that there is a movie screen in front of your eyes. You can recall your past and project it onto the screen."

2. "Think back to a really happy day. You can see yourself waking up in the bedroom you had at the time. Do you remember what your bed looked like? Did you share the room with anyone? Was there a window? Now imagine yourself waking up and getting ready for school. You wash up, get dressed, and eat breakfast."

3. "Now pretend that you have just arrived at school. Think of a day when your teacher said something nice to you. What did he or she say? What grade were you in? Can you remember a day that you completed some work that you were proud of? Can you remember how it felt when you turned that work in?"

4. "Now it is this year and you are in the _____ grade. This year you have a good friend. Give your friend a name. Is your friend a boy or a girl? Your friend likes you a lot and wants to do a lot of things with you. You enjoy doing things together. Your friend really likes school. Your friend gets very good grades and is liked by everyone. Teachers say that your friend is an ideal student. But your friend isn't a nerd—your friend is also on the basketball team and plays guitar in a band."

5. "Every day, when you and your friend go into the classroom together, your friend sits right down in his or her seat. Your friend always has paper and pencil ready. When the teacher gives an assignment, your friend immediately opens the book and begins to work. When it's time to go to the next class, your friend has completed the assignment and feels happy about finishing the work and not having it hanging over his or her head. When there's a test, your friend always studies for it."

6. "Now put yourself in your imaginary friend's shoes. *Be* your friend. It's time to go to the movies, and *you* have finished all your work. Your teacher is passing out report cards. She smiles at you and says, 'Congratulations, you have really worked hard this grading period. You earned these good grades.' You feel so free, so proud of the job you've done. You know that you did your best and that it was worth it. Give yourself a pat on the back, and then slowly open your eyes."

7. Discuss reactions to the guided imagery.

   a. Ask, "Could you imagine yourself as a good student? What did it feel like? What parts were hard to imagine?" Try to include all group members in the discussion.

   b. Say, "Two weeks ago, we talked about the goals you all have for your careers and about how doing well in school can help you achieve those goals. Last week, we also took a trip to a college. This week, we're going to talk about the things that you can do now to help you do well in school and feel good about it, like in the guided imagery."

Discussion of Being a Good Student

Advantages of Being a Good Student
Ask, "Why be a good student?" Pull for the following points:

1. Being a good student gives you more options for future careers that you would enjoy.

2. Being a good student and getting more schooling usually means you will make more money.

3. Being a good student allows you to participate in sports and other fun activities.

4. Being a good student makes your family happy.

5. Being a good student stops teachers from yelling at you.

Disadvantages of Being a Good Student
Ask, "Are there some negative things about being a good student?" Pull for the following points:

1. Being a good student may make you feel different than your friends.

2. You may be teased by your friends or brothers and sisters.

3. If you study, you may miss out on some time hanging out with friends.

Discussion of Goals

Discuss goal sheets passed out in Session One of Educational Aspirations.

1. Ask, **"Who brought back their My Goals sheets?**

    a. Give the promised candy or sticker to those who brought back completed sheets.

    b. Pass out goal sheets to anyone who forgot, and allow time for students to fill out the sheets.

2. Ask, **"What are your goals for this school year?"**

    a. Divide large paper into two columns. Write each student's goal on the left side of the paper.

    b. Ask each student, **"What do you need to do to reach this goal?"**

      (1) Write down the good student behaviors next to the goal.

      (2) If the student does not know what is necessary to reach the goal, ask the other students—for example, **"What could Silvia do to reach the goal of getting no D's or F's this semester?"**

3. Ask for a commitment to the steps necessary to reach the goal—for example, **"Silvia, can you commit to doing homework every night it is given for the rest of the semester?"**

4. Let students know you will be checking with them next week on how they are doing with the good student behavior they chose.

Check-Out

Elicit general reactions to the group. Ask, **"How does it feel to commit to being a better student? Do you feel you will be able to or willing to carry out your commitment? What might get in your way?"**

Peer Pressure and Gangs

Goal To help students develop effective strategies for resisting peer pressure, including peer pressure to join gangs

Overview of Sessions

Session One: Peer Pressure

- *Purpose:* Help students develop strategies and skills for resisting peer pressure

- *Content:* (1) Situations and Strategies Posters, (2) Tag-Team Peer Pressure game, (3) costs and benefits of resisting peer pressure

Session Two: Gangs

- *Purpose:* Prevent or decrease gang membership

- *Content:* (1) Positive and negative aspects of gang involvement, (2) different ways than gangs to get the advantages

Session One: Peer Pressure

Activities

- ✔ Check-in
- ✔ Follow-up on good student behaviors
- ✔ Situations and Strategies posters
- ✔ Tag-Team Peer Pressure game
- ✔ Costs and benefits of resisting peer pressure
- ✔ Check-out

Materials

- ✔ Curriculum
- ✔ A pad of paper large enough to be seen by all students

✔ Brightly colored pens

✔ Candy as reward for the game (optional)

✔ Resisting Peer Pressure handout (see Appendix B-5)

✔ Masking tape

✔ Rules and consequences with the group name at the top of the rules and consequences pages. Put these up in the room before each session.

Content

Check-In

Follow-Up on Good Student Behaviors

Check how students did with the good student behavior to which they committed last week. Ask, **"Who was able to do the good student behavior they committed to last week? How did it feel to accomplish that goal?"** Make sure to give lots of praise to those who were successful in their good student behavior. For those who did not complete their good student behavior, discuss obstacles that may have come up and generate solutions for overcoming the obstacles. Ensure that each student makes a commitment to their original or modified good student behavior for the next week as well.

Generate Peer Pressure Situations and Strategies Posters

The goal is to help students become aware of situations in which they may give in to peer pressure and to generate acceptable alternative strategies to "going along with the crowd."

Situations Poster
Group members are asked to generate situations in which they might encounter peer pressure. Say, **"Today we are going to talk about peer pressure. What is peer pressure? What are some situations in which people encounter peer pressure? When do people try to talk you into doing something that you don't know if you should do? I'll write the situations down on this poster."**

1. Write the situations on a poster labeled "Peer Pressure Situations."

2. The following are situations commonly listed by middle-school and high-school students (in no particular order). If members fail to mention one that you feel is important, ask, **"What about _____? Has anyone ever been pressured to _____?"**

    a. Ditching class.

    b. Fighting.

    c. Drugs.

    d. Stealing or shoplifting.

e. Gangs.

f. Cheating.

g. Picking on other kids.

h. Sex.

Strategies Poster

Group members are asked to generate strategies to resist peer pressure. Say **"Now that we have some peer pressure situations, let's try to think of ways to resist peer pressure."**

1. Write the strategies on a poster labeled "Peer Pressure Resistance Strategies."

2. Common strategies generated are listed below. As with the situations, ask questions to elicit the following strategies if they are not brought up by group members.

   a. Saying no.

   b. Changing the subject.

   c. Walking away or ignoring the person.

   d. Avoiding situations where they might encounter pressure.

   e. Hanging around with people who set good examples and who don't exert peer pressure on them.

   f. Identifying a person to whom they can talk when they feel pressured.

Peer Pressure Activity: Tag-Team Peer Pressure Game

The goal of this game is to allow students behavioral practice in using strategies to resist peer pressure. This activity is a verbal version of tag-team wrestling (in which two people wrestle and are relieved by partners who tag in when things get tough). The activity involves the following steps: (1) group members are divided into two teams, and each team chooses a captain; (2) you assign the role of 'pressurer' (the person pressuring the other) to one captain, and the role of 'pressuree' (the person getting pressured) to the other captain (or the captains can choose their roles); (3) the pressurer picks a peer pressure situation from the Situations poster and tries to pressure the pressuree; (4) the pressuree selects resistance strategies from the Strategies poster and tries to resist the pressurer; (5) the pressurer's team gets a point if the pressurer successfully pressures the pressuree into doing the activity, while the pressuree's team gets a point if he or she successfully resists; (6) the other team members can tag in for the pressurer or the pressuree if they're having difficulties pressuring or resisting.

1. Say, **"For this game, we need to divide into two teams and have each team pick a captain. Let's do that now so we can start the game."** After teams and captains are picked, say, **"This game is called the Tag-Team Peer Pressure game. Can anyone tell me what 'tag-team' means?"** Discuss their responses in

relation to the activity. "**In this game, one person from each team comes into the ring.**

a. "**One person is the pressurer. This person tries to pressure the other person to do one of the things on our list of situations. If the pressurer succeeds in getting the other person to do it, the pressurer's team gets the point.**

b. "**The other person is the pressuree. This person tries to resist the pressurer by using the strategies we listed or any other strategy—whatever is needed to resist. If the pressuree successfully resists, that team gets the point.**"

2. *Tagging-in.* "**The tag-team part comes in if one person is having a hard time. For example, if it looks like the pressuree is about to give in, a teammate can tag in for the pressuree and take over. On the other hand, if the pressurer is not having much success pressuring, a teammate can tag in and take over. OK, any questions? Ready to begin? Let's have the captain from each team begin. Which one wants to be the pressurer and which the pressuree?**" If you feel it would work better, you can assign the roles of pressurer and pressuree. For example, it is sometimes hard for a shy or passive student to start out as the pressuree because he or she may give in too quickly.

3. *Picking a situation.* Say, "**OK, [pressurer's name], you're the pressurer. What situation are you going to use to try to pressure [pressuree's name]? Look on the list and see which one you want to use. OK, now go ahead and try to pressure him or her. [Pressuree's name], remember, you can use any of the strategies on our resistance strategy list, or any other strategy as well. Team members, don't forget to tag-in if your teammate needs help or if you have a good idea. Good luck.**" If there is a disagreement about who should get a particular point, you should be the referee and decide who gets it, explaining specifically which behaviors led to the decision, or declare a tie.

4. *Rewards* (optional). If rewards are used, generally each member of the winning team gets two pieces of candy, and each member of the losing team gets one piece.

Evaluating Costs and Benefits of Resisting Peer Pressure

The goal of this discussion is to consider whether students can use some of these strategies themselves and to examine potential obstacles to using resistance strategies.

1. Say, "**Great job. Seems that it was pretty hard to resist some of those things. What are some reasons that it's sometimes hard to resist peer pressure in real life?**" (Uncool, afraid of rejection, etc.) "**Which of these strategies do you think might work in real life? Which ones have you tried, and how did they work?**"

2. Hand out Resisting Peer Pressure sheets. Say, "**We'd like you to notice one situation over the next week where your friends pressure you to do something.**

See if you can resist the pressure, and next week we'll talk about what strategies you used to resist and how they worked."

Check-Out

Elicit general responses to the session. Ask, **"What did you learn that might be useful to you about resisting peer pressure?"** Remind students to notice a situation when they are pressured and to reflect on how they responded.

Session Two: Gangs

(If gangs are not a threat or reality in a particular school, this session may be omitted.)

Activities
- ✔ Check-in
- ✔ Follow-up on Resisting Peer Pressure handout
- ✔ Discussion of group members' gang involvement and knowledge
- ✔ Advantages and disadvantages of joining gangs
- ✔ Different ways than gangs to get the advantages
- ✔ Check-out

Materials
- ✔ Curriculum
- ✔ A pad of paper large enough to be seen by all students
- ✔ Brightly colored pens
- ✔ Masking tape
- ✔ Rules and consequences with the group name at the top of the rules and consequences pages. Put these up in the room before each session.

Content

Check-In

Follow-Up on Resisting Peer Pressure Handout

Pressure Situations
Say, "Remember from last week that you were going to notice when friends pressured you about something? Who can share an example of when that happened to them? Who else has examples?"

Resistance Strategies
Ask, "**Who tried to resist the pressure? How did you do it?**" Ask members for examples of how they tried to resist. Also ask if members decided not to resist the pressure, and what made them give in to it.

Evaluating the Outcome
Ask, "**How did you feel about resisting the pressure (or giving in to the pressure)?**" Be accepting of their answers, discussing again the costs and benefits of resisting peer pressure.

Discussion of Group Members' Gang Involvement and Knowledge

Say, "**This week we are going to talk about gangs.**" If appropriate, say, "**This topic has come up before, and several of you have mentioned knowing people in gangs or being in a gang yourself. We know this topic can be hard to talk about, but we want you to know that we will not judge you if you are in a gang or know people who are. Also, remember that everyone must keep everything said in the group confidential. We know that there are a lot of reasons that people join gangs, and we want to talk about some of the advantages and disadvantages of being in gangs. We'd like to start by talking about experiences you may have had, both positive and negative, with gangs. Is anyone in a gang or has anyone had an experience with gangs?**" In facilitating this discussion, it is important to be neutral and nonevaluative about gang involvement.

Advantages and Disadvantages of Joining Gangs

Advantages
Say, "**Now we're going to talk about the reasons people join gangs. What are some advantages of being in gangs? What can people get out of being in a gang?**"

1. Often respect, admiration, love, support, and safety and security are mentioned.

2. Write the reasons on a large piece of paper labeled "Advantages of Gangs."

Disadvantages
Say, "**What are some reasons not to join gangs? What are some disadvantages of belonging to gangs?**"

1. Getting killed and killing are often included on this list.

2. Write the reasons on another large piece of paper labeled "Disadvantages of Gangs."

Brainstorming Different Ways to Obtain Advantages That Gangs Provide

Say, "**There seem to be some important advantages and disadvantages to joining gangs. It seems like the cost can be very high if you join a gang. What if you decide not to join a gang? It still seems like you would want some of the** advantages we talked about before. [Point to advantages poster.] **What are some other ways of getting these important things besides being in a gang?"**

1. Sports (respect, admiration).

2. Family and extended family (love, support).

3. After-school clubs, church groups (love, support).

4. A trusted adult, big brother, school security guard, and so on (security, support).

Check-Out

Elicit general reactions to the session? Ask, **"What are some other ways besides being in a gang that you personally can get some of the advantages?"**

Exposure to Community Violence and Posttraumatic Stress Reactions

Goal To help students share their experiences as victims or witnesses of violence; to normalize and understand posttraumatic stress

Overview of Sessions

Session One
- *Purpose:* Facilitation of discussion of exposure to violence and related feelings
- *Content:* Scary art gallery

Session Two (if needed to continue processing drawings and feelings; necessary for groups with high violence exposure)
- *Purpose:* Introduction of concept of posttraumatic stress
- *Content:* (1) Continuation of scary art gallery (if needed), (2) posttraumatic stress discussion and game

Session One

Activities
- ✔ Check-in
- ✔ Preparation for termination
- ✔ Scary art gallery
- ✔ Check-out

Materials
- ✔ Curriculum
- ✔ One piece of blank drawing paper for each student, plus some extras

✔ Brightly colored pens

✔ Masking tape

✔ Rules and consequences with the group name at the top of the rules and consequences pages. Put these up in the room before each session.

Content

Check-In

Preparation for Termination

It is important to discuss the ending of the group early so that students can have a chance to reflect on and express any feelings they may be having. These may include feelings of regret about having to go back to class, missing group leaders or other students, or being happy that summer is coming. Goals are (1) to help students feel some control over the process of ending the group by accepting and validating all feelings about termination; (2) to help members reflect on the gains they have made by pointing out changes they have noticed; (3) to provide an opportunity for group members to bring up any topics they wished had been covered and would like to address in the last weeks of the group.

Say, "**We only have about three more groups left after today, and I am wondering what feelings you have about the group ending.**" Elicit responses. If it is hard for group members to respond, you can share your own feelings about the ending of the groups (e.g., feeling attached to them or knowing you will miss them; being pleased with the changes you've seen and with their hard work; having enjoyed the group). "**OK. We'll talk more about our feelings about ending in the next few weeks, and we'll also plan our party. It's something we like to talk about now so that the end of the group doesn't sneak up and surprise us.**"

Exposure to Violence Activity: Scary Art Gallery

The goal is to allow students to graphically display traumatic experiences in their lives. This activity includes the following steps: (1) Students draw the scariest thing that ever happened to them; (2) drawings are posted in the art gallery; (3) students describe the event to the other group members; (4) students process feelings, fantasies, and prevention strategies. Representative student drawings are shown on pages 72–76.

1. Give each group member a piece of paper and different-colored markers.

2. Introduce the activity by saying, "**Today we're going to do an activity called scary art gallery. Think of the scariest thing that has happened to you. These should be things that have really happened to you, not things that you are scared of like Chuckie from a movie. A lot of scary things happen every day. For example, people are killed, fires happen, people are beat up.**" [If appropriate, add, "**Several of you have already talked about times that you have seen or been the victims of violent events.**"] You can draw the situ-

ation with stick figures if you'd like. The important thing is not how nice your drawing looks, but that you are able to draw about something important to you. It should be something serious—this isn't a funny subject."

3. Give students time to draw their pictures.

4. Tape students' drawings on the wall to exhibit them in the gallery. When all are completed, students should sit facing the gallery.

5. Ask members to describe the event in their drawing. Say, "**Looks like you all drew about some pretty scary and important things. Now we'd like each of you to tell the group about what is in your drawing and how you felt when it happened.**" For each presentation, make sure to deal with the following issues:

   a. *Feelings.* "**How did you feel when that happened?**" (If the student is unable to share his or her feelings, the leader can reflect the feelings—e.g., "**That must have been really upsetting or scary; you must have felt so helpless.**")

   b. *Fantasies.* "**That's a scary situation. Sometimes people imagine ways they would have liked to act that wouldn't be possible in real life because they're too dangerous. Is there anything that you would have liked to do in that situation to make it better if you had super powers?**"

   c. *Empowerment strategies.* "**There's no way to totally prevent what happened, but is there any way you can think of to help keep yourself safe if this happens again (or reduce the likelihood of it happening again)?**" If the student cannot think of any safety strategies, ask for input from other group members: "**Can anyone think of something [student's name] could do to prevent this from happening again or to keep safe if it does happen?**"

   d. *Shared experience.* "**Has anyone else been in a situation like this or had something like this happen to them?**"

6. Sometimes the intensity of some disclosures causes anxiety in the group. If this is expressed by inattention or laughter or silliness, it is important to comment that when scary stuff is being discussed, sometimes it makes people nervous and they have trouble listening.

7. This activity, with the full discussion, may take more than one session. If so, finish up during the next session. Especially in groups with high community and/or family violence exposure, it is important for students to be able to discuss their experiences fully.

Check-Out

Elicit general feelings about the session. If a great deal of emotion or very difficult disclosures have occurred, reflect the feelings of the group: "**Several students shared very difficult experiences and feelings today; sometimes it was hard, but I think we all appreciate their openness and willingness to share.**"

Students' Scary Art Gallery drawings (re-creations of actual drawings)

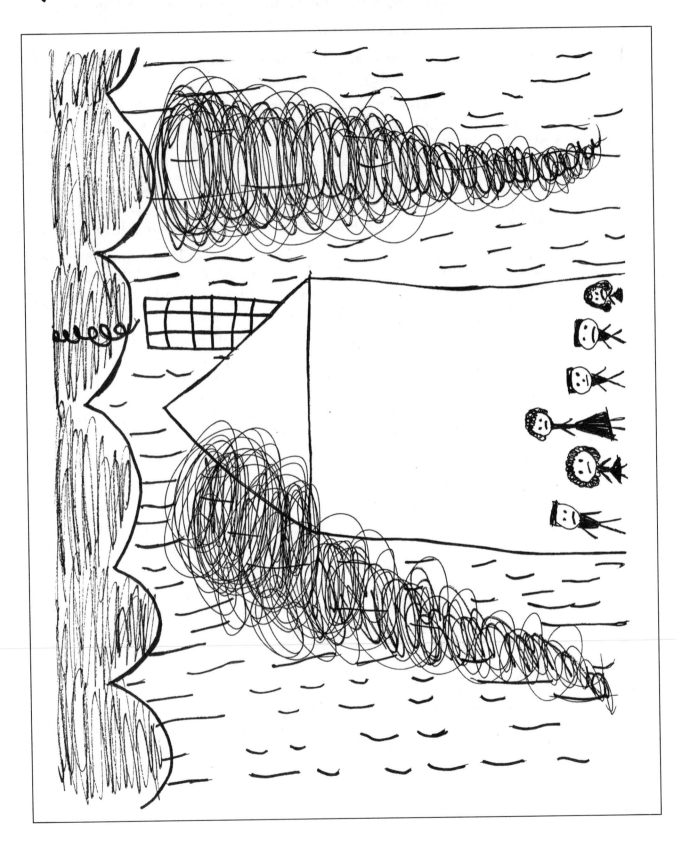

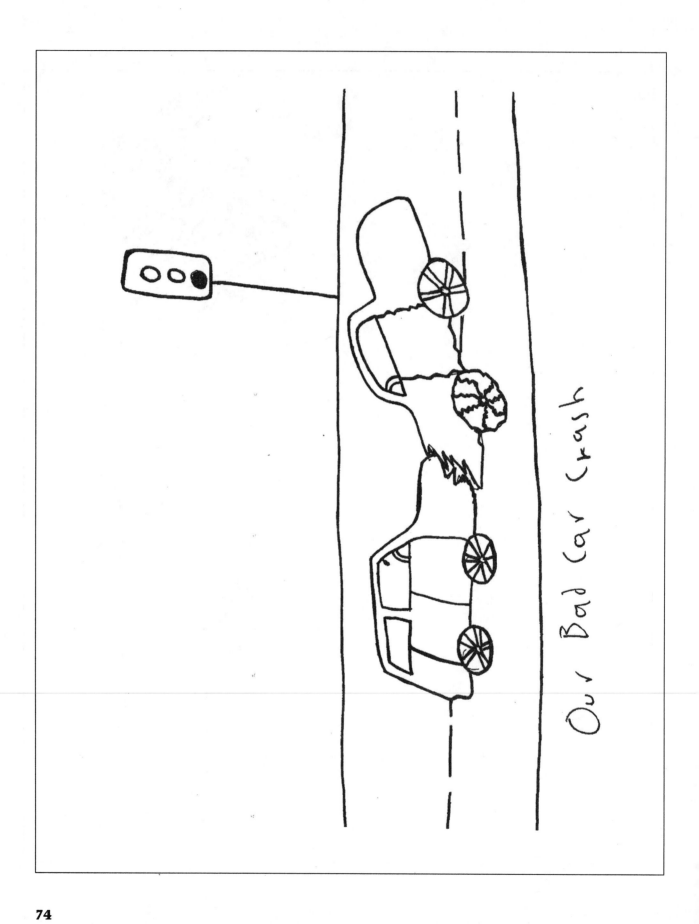

Our Bad Car Crash

Session Two

(Optional for groups without high violence exposure; necessary for groups with high violence exposure.)

Activities
- ✔ Check-in
- ✔ Finish scary art gallery (if not completed last session)
- ✔ Posttraumatic stress reactions discussion and game
- ✔ Check-out

Materials
- ✔ Curriculum
- ✔ Scary art gallery drawings from Session One (post these on the wall)
- ✔ Posttraumatic Stress Reactions handout (one copy for each student—see Appendix B-6a)
- ✔ Disks for posttraumatic stress reactions activity (50 copies of each of the three types of disks with each type a different color—see Appendix B-6b)
- ✔ Candy to exchange for disks at the end of the session (optional)
- ✔ Masking tape
- ✔ Rules and consequences with the group name at the top of the rules and consequences pages. Put these up in the room before each session.

Content

Check-In

Scary Art Gallery (continued from last week)

If some group members need to finish presenting or discussing their drawings, continue with the scary art gallery exhibit until completed. Follow the instructions in Session One.

Exposure to Violence Activity: Posttraumatic Stress Reactions Handout and Discussion

The goal is to help students learn about common reactions to trauma that they may have had, to help them understand why these reactions occur, and to develop strategies to deal with the reactions.

Introducing the Concept of Posttraumatic Stress

Say (if appropriate), "We saw from people's drawings in scary art gallery that many frightening and traumatic things have happened to group members—like hearing shots, seeing someone stabbed or beaten, or having it happen to you. We now know that when such horrible things happen to people, they tend to react in certain ways to try to cope. These are totally normal reactions to abnormal events. They are called posttraumatic stress reactions. Has anyone ever heard of that? We're going to give you a handout with the different types of reactions that people have after something traumatic happens, then play a game to see which of these reactions you may have had."

Posttraumatic Stress Reaction Clusters

Say, "There are three basic categories of reactions. Some people who have been exposed to a trauma will have only one type, some will have reactions of all types. Many of you may have been exposed to lots of violence and trauma, which makes these reactions more likely."

1. "The first category is *reexperiencing the trauma.* We're going to talk about each way people may reexperience the trauma. If that has happened to you, tell us your experience, and you will get a reexperiencing token."

    a. "Having memories or thoughts of the bad thing that happened suddenly pop into your mind." Ask students if this has ever happened to them. Ask for specific examples, and give a green reexperiencing token to each person who gives a personal example.

    b. "Dreaming about what happened over and over." Ask students if this has ever happened to them. Ask for specific examples, and give a green reexperiencing token to each person who gives a personal example.

    c. "Having the feeling that the traumatic event is happening again, like flashbacks." Ask students if this has ever happened to them. Ask for specific examples, and give a green reexperiencing token to each person who gives a personal example.

    d. "Getting really nervous or uncomfortable if you get near the place where the bad thing happened." Ask students if this has ever happened to them. Ask for specific examples, and give a green reexperiencing token to each person who gives a personal example.

2. "The second category is *avoiding* stuff about the traumatic thing, or *feeling numb.* We'll talk about the different ways people cope by avoiding anything that reminds them of the bad thing or avoiding feelings. If that has happened to you, tell us your experience, and you will get an avoiding token."

    a. "Avoiding people, places, or activities that remind you of the bad thing that happened." Ask students if this has ever happened to them. Ask for specific examples, and give an orange avoiding token to each person who gives a personal example.

    b. **"Feeling detached or cut off from other people or numb."** Ask students if this has ever happened to them. Ask for specific examples, and give an orange avoiding token to each person who gives a personal example.

    c. **"Being less interested and involved in things you liked to do before the bad thing happened."** Ask students if this has ever happened to them. Ask for specific examples, and give an orange avoiding token to each person who gives a personal example.

    d. **"Thinking you won't have a career or a family or that you will die young."** Ask students if this has ever happened to them. Ask for specific examples, and give an orange avoiding token to each person who gives a personal example.

3. **"The third category is** *feeling more on edge* **than you did before the bad things happened. We'll talk about the different ways people might feel more on edge. If that has happened to you, tell us your experience, and you will get an edge token."**

    a. **"Trouble falling asleep or staying asleep."** Ask students if this has ever happened to them. Ask for specific examples, and give a purple edge token to each person who gives a personal example.

    b. **"Being irritable or getting angry easily."** Ask students if this has ever happened to them. Ask for specific examples, and give a purple edge token to each person who gives a personal example.

    c. **"Getting distracted and having trouble paying attention."** Ask students if this has ever happened to them. Ask for specific examples, and give a purple edge token to each person who gives a personal example.

    d. **"Being super-aware of where danger might be, or startling easily."** Ask students if this has ever happened to them. Ask for specific examples, and give a purple edge token to each person who gives a personal example.

Identifying Typical Patterns of Reacting

Say, **"We can see that these posttraumatic stress reactions happen to everybody and are part of coping with bad things that happen to us or that we see happen. You can tell from the colors of your tokens which types of reactions you yourself have. What color tokens did you have the most of?"**

Have students tell their ratios of tokens. The goal is for them to recognize their typical patterns of reaction. For example, **"So Juan, you have more purple tokens than green and orange combined. So what are the ways you have learned to react to traumatic things?"** Wait for his answer. Or elicit an answer from other group members if he does not know, then restate: **"That's right, you tend to get on edge—you can't sleep well and get angry easily."**

Why Identify Ways of Reacting to Trauma?

Say, **"Why do you think it might be important to know how each of us reacts when faced with bad and traumatic things?"** Elicit their reactions and shape them to make the following points:

1. It helps us understand otherwise puzzling reactions and see them as normal reactions to abnormal events.

2. If we know why we feel these ways, it gives us choices to act differently than we usually do. For example, if I know I feel nothing because I'm avoiding feelings about my brother getting shot, I need to allow myself to feel the feelings of grief about his death that I'm avoiding. Or if I get angry at every little thing, I probably need to recognize that I'm still in a rage about what happened to my cousin, and not take it out on everyone around me who had nothing to do with what happened to my cousin.

3. We can actively do things to try to minimize having even more trauma (e.g., don't hang around gang members, know where to go in school if you feel unsafe).

Check-Out

Elicit general reactions to the group. Ask how they feel they might use what they learned about their reactions to trauma. Give members one or two small pieces of candy in exchange for their tokens.

Family Relationships

This module may be expanded to two sessions.

Goal   Understanding and accepting one's family

Overview of Session

Session One
- *Purpose:* Sharing feelings about one's family; working toward acceptance of families

- *Content:* (1) Family Me Too game; (2) Personality Family Album game; (3) ideal family movie

Session One

(May be expanded to two sessions.)

Activities
- ✔ Check-in
- ✔ Planning for termination
- ✔ Family Me Too game
- ✔ Personality Family Album game
- ✔ Ideal family movie
- ✔ Assessing family support
- ✔ Check-out

Materials
- ✔ Curriculum
- ✔ Masking tape

✔ Rules and consequences with the group name at the top of the rules and consequences pages. Put these up in the room before each session.

Content

Check-In

Planning for Termination

Discussion of Termination

Given that this is the next to last session, it is important to again bring up feelings about the ending of the group. The goals are to help students share their feelings about the ending and to point out positive changes they (or you) have noticed about individual members or about the group as a whole (e.g., more trusting, more able to talk about difficult topics). Remember that it is fine to share your own feelings if that feels comfortable. Refer back to Module Six, Session One, for other ideas about discussing termination.

Planning the Party

Say, **"It's clear that people have lots of feelings about the group ending. In our last session, we'd like to celebrate our group with a party. Who has ideas about what we should bring to eat and drink?"**

1. Solicit ideas about food and drink. In very poor schools, the leaders generally supply the refreshments. If there are budgetary constraints, it is fine to set guidelines, such as **"Do you guys prefer cookies, cupcakes, or chips and dip?"** In other schools or groups, group members want to volunteer to bring food for the party; if so, it is useful to give each student a card with what they chose to bring on it to help them remember to bring it next week.

2. Students sometimes suggest bringing decorations or having music, and these generally add to the party atmosphere. However, there is an important termination activity, so it is not a good idea to plan to watch a movie or play games, since the time is generally limited to one school period. The party parameters should be set to meet the needs and resources of the particular group, leader, and school.

Family Relationship Activity: Family Me Too Game

The goal of all the activities in this module is to help group members speak about family issues, some of which may have been discussed in previous modules and some of which will be new. The idea is to illustrate that everyone has feelings about and problems related to family and that it may help to share these feelings.

1. Say, **"Today we're going to talk about our families. Our first activity is going to help us look at the things we like and things we wish were different about our families. Does anyone remember the game we played on our first day of the group?"** Wait for response. **"That's right, we played the Me Too**

game. Today we're going to play the same game, only instead of saying things about ourselves, we're going to say things about our families that we like and that we wish were different. Remember that you want to say things that you think other people will have in common with you."

2. **"Let's start with things we like about our family."** Examples are: "My mom is a really good cook," "My brother helps me with hard homework," or "My mom almost always listens when I have a problem." Leaders may need to model responses to begin the activity.

3. After 5 or 10 minutes, say, **"Now let's switch to things we wish were different about our family."** Examples are: "My dad never has time for me," "My sister always takes my things without asking," or "My mom yells at me all the time." Spend another 5 to 10 minutes on this. (See Module One, Session One to review the Me Too game).

Family Relationship Activity: Personality Family Album

The goal of this activity is to help students connect with personality characteristics they share in common with family members. Say, **"Next, let's talk about ways our families have influenced us. Family members have a strong influence on our personalities and the way we act. We hardly ever stop and think about the ways our families shape our personalities and make us the way we are. So now we're going to play a game called Personality Family Album. We're going to go around the circle and ask each of you to describe two qualities that you have in common with someone else in your family (e.g., just like your mother, father, sister . . .). We'd like one of these qualities to be one that you like and one that you don't like. Also describe how it makes you feel to have those qualities. I'll start to show you how it's played (e.g., I get my sense of humor from my dad, and I like that. I get my temper from my mom, and I don't like that. My sister is a brat, and sometimes I am too)."** Go around the circle so that each student takes a turn. When appropriate, ask the other group members whether they have similar feelings and reactions about their own families.

Family Relationship Activity: Ideal Family Movie

The final family relationship activity is meant to help students think about how they would like their families to be. Say, **"We can choose our friends, but we don't get to pick our families. Our next activity is called ideal family movie. If you were going to make a movie about your family, and you were the writer and the director so you could make it the way you really wanted your family to be, what would you change about your family for the movie?"**

1. If students suggest changes that are reasonable (e.g., "My mom would spend more time with me; my sister and I wouldn't fight all the time"), wonder

   a. What might happen if the student asked for the changes.

   b. Whether there is something the student might do to help this change take place.

2. If they suggest changes that are not realistic (e.g., "My dad wasn't in jail; my mom would stop taking drugs; my parents would get back together again"), reflect the student's feelings with an empathic comment (e.g., "You miss your dad and it's really upsetting that he's in jail; it's been 6 years, and you still wish that your parents would get together again").

Assessing Family Support

Ask students who they can go to in their families for help when they have a problem or when they are upset. How do they ask for help? Have group members give suggestions to any students who don't know who to go to for help or support or how to ask for help. If a student feels that no one in the family could understand or help, try to identify another adult they trust and to whom they could go for help.

Check-Out

Elicit general reactions about the session. Ask, **"Did you notice any patterns about families from our activities?"** Remind students that next session will be the last group.

Termination Session: The Party

Activities

- ✔ Trust ratings
- ✔ Check-in
- ✔ Party—eat treats and talk socially
- ✔ Group memories
- ✔ What I like about you
- ✔ Certificates
- ✔ Check-out

Materials

- ✔ Curriculum
- ✔ Trust ratings (one for each student—see Appendix B-1a)
- ✔ Treats (see last session for hints about this)
- ✔ What I Like about You sheets (one for each student—see Appendix B-7a)
- ✔ Certificates (one for each student—see Appendix B-7b for a sample)
- ✔ Colored markers
- ✔ Masking tape
- ✔ Rules and consequences with the group name at the top of the rules and consequences pages. Put these up in the room before each session.

Content

Trust Ratings

As students come in, ask them to fill out another trust rating.

Check-In

This is usually informal over treats.

Party

Eat treats and enjoy group members.

Process Group Memories

Discuss group members' experience of the group. Say, **"We've done a lot of things together over the last 15 weeks. We're wondering what kinds of things you liked or found difficult. What special things do you think you'll remember from the group?"** Process reactions. Group leaders can share their experiences as well (i.e., unique things they have learned from the group or group members, effect group has had on them, reasons they will not forget the group members).

Termination Activity: What I Like about You

The goal of this final activity is to focus on positive connections between group members and to leave the members with a written reminder of their own special qualities. Say, **"Our last activity is to make a souvenir for each of you. It's so easy to give put-downs, but we rarely take the time to give put-ups. So today we're going to concentrate on put-ups. I have a sheet for each of you. We'll go around the circle, and each person will say one nice thing that they like about you. I will write these on your sheet, and you can take it home at the end of the group. Who wants to begin?"** Wait for a volunteer. **"Great! What color do you want your name written in? OK, we'll start with [name of student to left of volunteer]. What's one nice thing you like about [name of volunteer]?"** Write each statement on the sheet, then give it to the student.

1. You also participate in giving put-ups, but you do not usually have sheets written about you. If students really want to do put-up sheets for you, then it should be allowed.

2. Sometimes, students will say mean things. Refocus them on something nice that they like about the student. Ask, **"Is that a put-up? Think of something positive that you like about _____."**

3. Sometimes, students will say things that may be taken as mean or nice. If this happens, ask the target student if he or she thinks it's nice and wants it written down. "Loudmouthed" is an example of this ambiguous category. If it does not feel like a put-up to the target student, ask the person giving feedback to pick something else that they like about the person.

Distribute Certificates

Check-Out

Elicit general reactions to the group. Help students say good-bye. Sometimes groups will want to have a reunion in a few months. This can serve as a booster session to reinforce major concepts discussed in the groups (e.g., hot-headed vs. cool-headed responses, problem-solving strategies, talking about feelings and responding empathically, dealing with traumatic events). Be sure to say your own goodbyes to students. Some members want to hug you—this is fine if you are comfortable with it.

Congratulate yourself for completing the SPARK program!

CHAPTER THREE

Effectiveness of SPARK Groups

In this section, we will first describe the characteristics of the hundreds of adolescents who have already participated in the SPARK groups, based on individual pregroup interviews, and we will then discuss the demonstrated effectiveness of the SPARK group curriculum, comparing time 1 (pregroup) and time 2 (postgroup) interview responses.

Characteristics of Participating Group Members

All of the students who participated in SPARK are from urban schools in the Los Angeles area, including six public middle schools and two public high schools. Among group members, there were more middle-school than high-school participants and more boys than girls. Students were primarily African American and Latino.

Family Structure and Distress

Participants in the SPARK program typically did not come from intact families. Although 37% lived with both parents, 51% lived with just one parent, and 12% lived with neither parent (most frequently living with other relatives or less frequently in a foster home). Participating youth also reported high rates of family distress. For example, in our sample, 37% reported having a family member in jail or prison; 27% reported that a family member had a drug and/or alcohol

	Percentage
Grade level	
6th	30%
7th	25%
8th	30%
9th	14%
10th or higher	2%
Gender	
Male	60%
Female	40%
Ethnicity	
African American	49%
Latino/Latina	39%
Mixed/other	12%

problem; 10% had parents who divorced in the previous year; 26% were bothered by their parents' arguing with one another; and 39% were bothered by arguments with their parents.

Exposure to Community Violence

In addition to family distress, participants in the SPARK program reported alarmingly high rates of exposure to community violence. For example, 42% had seen someone being killed, and 9% had been shot or shot at with a gun. Percentages of those exposed to violence are given in the chart on the next page.

We have found that exposure to community violence is associated with numerous emotional, cognitive, and behavioral conse-

Violent event	Percentage
Chased by gangs	22%
Beaten up or mugged	14%
Attacked or stabbed with a knife	6%
Shot or shot at with a gun	9%
House broken into when at home	11%
Saw someone carrying a gun or knife	55%
Heard a gun fired while at home	62%
Saw someone being killed	42%

quences. For example, among youth in the SPARK groups, exposure to community violence is significantly linked with increased psychological distress, including depression, anxiety, and posttraumatic stress. Adolescents with more exposure to violence also have significantly lower levels of self-esteem. Finally, exposure to community violence is significantly linked with increased physical aggression (i.e., hitting, kicking, and slapping others) and gang involvement (i.e., having friends in a gang, believing it is necessary to be in a gang). These findings are consistent with other samples of inner-city youth around the country.

Outcomes of the SPARK Groups

To examine the effectiveness of the SPARK groups, information collected from 241 students before the groups began (time 1) was compared with information from their interviews after the groups ended (time 2). In addition, information from these 241 students was compared to information from 78 students who were initially placed in a wait-list control group. Of course, students in the wait-list control group were subsequently placed in SPARK groups, and they were interviewed again after they had completed the groups. Hence, students in the control group were interviewed on three occasions: twice before the groups began and once after the groups ended.

Time 1 and Time 2 Differences for Those in the Treatment Group

Those in the treatment group reported significant gains in a number of areas. After participating in the SPARK groups, the adolescents had significantly higher educational aspirations, and, although their math grades did not change significantly, they did achieve significantly higher English grades (see Figure 1). Additionally, those in the treatment group reported significant gains in self-esteem and in psychological adjustment, including decreased anxiety, depression, and posttraumatic stress. Finally, those in the treatment group felt significantly more attached and connected to their peers following participation in the SPARK groups.

After completing the groups, SPARK participants were also asked to complete a brief satisfaction survey. In general, the participants agreed that they "got a lot out of counseling," and that counseling helped them feel better about themselves and do better in school. Additionally, group leaders were asked to complete a brief evaluation for each student who participated. As part of the evaluation, group leaders were asked the question, "Overall, how much did this student benefit from the group?" Responses were given on a 5-point scale (i.e., 1 = not at all; 2 = mild; 3 = moderate; 4 = much;

Figure 1. English grades.

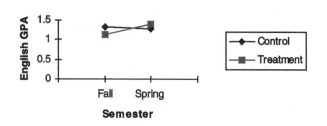

5 = very much). Altogether, group leaders indicated that 75% of students who completed the SPARK groups benefited "moderately," "much," or "very much."

Time 1 and Time 2 Differences for Those in the Control Group

Adolescents in the wait-list control group were interviewed at the same time as those in the treatment group. In general, from time 1 to time 2 (both before they participated in SPARK), those in the control group did not report the same gains as those in the treatment group. In fact, in comparing their time 1 and time 2 interviews, those in the control group reported a significant increase in gang involvement (i.e., number of friends in a gang). However, those in the control group did report a significant decrease in depression and alienation from peers.

Comparisons between the Treatment and Control Groups

Although we tried to randomly assign students to treatment and control groups, students in major distress were immediately placed in the treatment group. As a result, at time 1, adolescents in the treatment group were significantly more distressed in a number of areas when compared to those in the control group. In particular, adolescents in the treatment group had significantly lower levels of self-esteem, ethnic identity, peer attachment, and educational aspirations than those in the control group at time 1. At time 2, however, none of these differences were significant. Furthermore, when each student's time 1 score was taken into account, comparisons between time 2 scores indicated that those in the treatment group were significantly less likely to believe that it is necessary to be in a gang than those in the control group (see Figure 2).

Figure 2. Necessity of being in a gang.

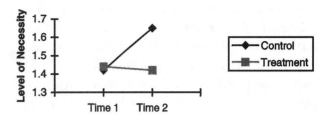

In addition to these gains, a doctoral student involved in the SPARK program found that the groups were effective in the area of perceived control. In particular, compared to those in the control group, students in the treatment group reported a decrease in their perceptions of external control (i.e., that their fate was in the hands of others). In addition, changes in perceived control were associated with increased educational aspirations and decreased aggressive behavior (Watt, 1998).

Summary and Conclusions

The SPARK group counseling curriculum has been implemented in a number of secondary schools in the Los Angeles area. In our groups, more males than females, more middle-school than high-school students, and primarily African American and Latino or Latina adolescents have participated. In general, participants did not come from intact families, and they reported alarmingly high rates of family distress and exposure to community violence. In turn, exposure to community violence was linked with numerous deleterious consequences, including psychological distress, lowered self-esteem, increased physical aggression, and gang involvement.

The SPARK curriculum appears to be effective in a number of domains, including academic goals and achievement, psychological adjustment, self-esteem, attachment to peers, and gang involvement. With respect to academics, group members report an increase in educational aspirations and also achieve significantly higher English grades following participation in the groups. With respect to psychological adjustment, following participation in the SPARK groups, members report significant decreases in anxiety, depression, and post-traumatic stress, as well as a significant increase in self-esteem. Participants also report increased attachment and connectedness to peers following the groups. Finally, compared to those in the control group, adolescents who participate in the groups are less likely to view gang involvement as necessary.

Although participants in the SPARK groups reported significant gains in a number of areas, the gains tended to be relatively modest. For example, although the students achieved significantly higher English grades following participation in the program, their grades were still quite poor. One possible explanation for the modest findings is that adolescents in our groups are particularly at risk; they all live in the inner-city, contending with such chronic stressors as poverty, community violence, and family distress. A second possible explanation involves treatment studies in general. Typically, treatment studies that are relatively brief and circumscribed yield modest results, especially those involving at-risk adolescents (see Kazdin, 1993). As in other treatment studies, we did not expect dramatic improvements, as such gains would most likely require a very intensive, multicomponent, long-term, and costly intervention. Our hope is that students will continue to make gains in the months and years following participation as they practice skills acquired through the program.

Contrary to our expectations, students who participated in the groups did not report a significant decrease in physical aggression despite an emphasis on anger management in the curriculum and despite group leader reports of students' increased use of cool-headed responses in a variety of situations. This is most likely due to the questionable validity of our measure of physical aggression (i.e., "How many times have you hit, kicked, or slapped someone in the last month?"). This one question is an inadequate measure of physical aggression; it was developed for this project, has statistical problems, and does not discriminate between sibling squabbles and serious interpersonal aggression. Given that significant gains were made in other areas (e.g., self-esteem, psychological adjustment) that were assessed with established and widely used measures, it is possible that we would have found significant results in the area of physical aggression had we used a more reliable and valid measure. We are now using a revised measure of physical aggression and have included a shortened version of our measure in the pre–post group interview (see Appendix A-5).

Overall, the groups yield benefits in a variety of areas, including academic achievement, psychological adjustment, self-esteem, peer connectedness and attachment, and alternatives to gang involvement. The SPARK group counseling curriculum is applicable to a wide variety of adolescents, including the general population as well as adolescents at high risk for developing severe behavioral, emotional, and/or academic problems.

Information Regarding Data Analyses

For more detailed information regarding the data analyses, please contact the authors through Jill Waterman, PhD, Department of Psychology, UCLA, 405 Hilgard Avenue, Los Angeles, CA 90095-1563.

Sample Materials for Beginning SPARK Groups

Permission to photocopy the forms in this appendix is granted to purchasers of this book for personal use only (see copyright page for details).

SPARK Counseling Groups Referral Form

SPARK counseling groups are for students who are currently experiencing academic, social, emotional, and/or family difficulties or have been exposed to high levels of violence. The groups will meet for one class period a week for 15 weeks. Topics covered in the groups include anger management, educational aspirations, family relationships, and peer pressure and gangs. If you know of a student who could benefit from such an experience and who can work cooperatively in a group, please refer him or her using the space below.

Student's Name: _____

Gender: _____

Grade: _____

Ethnicity: _____

Reason for Referral (please place an X next to all relevant concerns):

_____ **Family problems**

_____ **Disruptive or disobedient**

_____ **Inattentive**

_____ **Anxious or nervous**

_____ **Sad or withdrawn**

_____ **Academic problems**

_____ **Exposure to violence**

_____ **Other (please specify):** _____

Teacher's/Counselor's Name and Date: _____

Thank you for referring this student to the SPARK program. We will be contacting him or her in the next few days.

APPENDIX A-1   From Waterman and Walker (2000). Copyright 2000 by The Guilford Press.

Sample Script for Presenting SPARK Groups to Potential Group Members

1. Introduce yourself.

2. Explain the purpose of SPARK groups: "I'm here to talk to you about SPARK groups here at school. The groups are a place where kids come to talk about things that are going on in their lives—like things that happen at school or at home. We'll also be talking about certain things that are important to people your age. For example, we'll be talking about your future plans, ways to control anger, racism, and family relationships. Almost everything talked about in the group is confidential. This means that what happens in the group—what gets talked about—won't be shared with your parents, teachers, or friends."

3. Outline the structure of SPARK groups: "The groups meet for one class period every week for 15 weeks. Every time we meet, you'll have a chance to talk about what is going on in your life. In addition, we will have a fun activity that is related to the topic for that day. Later, we'll be taking an all-day field trip to a local university where you can learn more about college life. Before the group starts and after it ends, we will need to ask everyone who participates some questions. Responses to these questions will be kept private."

4. Explain why the child was referred to participate in the group: "The reason you've been invited here today is because someone, either a teacher or a school counselor, identified you as a person who works well with other students and who might like to be in this group. We've done a lot of these groups before and students seem to like them."

5. Answer any questions students might have.

6. Give a Parent Consent Form to each student who is interested in participating.

SPARK Parent Consent Form

What Are SPARK Groups?

SPARK counseling groups are for students who have been identified by school counselors or teachers as students who can work cooperatively in a group and who may benefit from this type of experience. For SPARK groups, students will miss one class period a week for a total of 15 weeks. In the group sessions, the following topics will be covered: trust building, anger management, problem solving, the importance of education for the future, ethnic pride, dealing with discrimination, avoiding peer pressure and gangs, family relationships, and coping with community violence. Specific activities will be presented in each session, and students will be encouraged to share their own feelings and experiences.

Students will be interviewed before and after participation in the groups. The interview contains questions about the student's feelings, attitudes and beliefs, experiences, level of stress, and problem behaviors.

Confidentiality

Students' responses to the interview questions and their participation in the SPARK groups will be kept confidential, except as required by law. The privilege of confidentiality does not extend to information about sexual, emotional, or physical abuse or neglect of a child. If the SPARK leader has reasonable suspicion or is given such information, the leader is required to report to the authorities. Also, if the SPARK leader believes that a student is at significant risk of harming himself or herself or someone else, the leader will need to ensure the student's safety by telling the child's parent or guardian and the school counselor.

Participation and Withdrawal

Participation in the interview and in the SPARK groups is voluntary. If a student does not participate, there will be no negative effects on the relationship with the school or in the classroom. The SPARK leader can be reached at the number below if any questions or concerns about the interview or the groups arise.

I give permission for my child to participate in SPARK groups, as described above. In signing this form, I acknowledge that I have received a copy of the consent form.

_____   _____
Parent's Signature and Date   **Student's Name**

_____   _____
SPARK Leader   **SPARK Leader's Phone Number**

APPENDIX A-3   From Waterman and Walker (2000). Copyright 2000 by The Guilford Press.

SPARK Student Assent Form

I am being invited to participate in SPARK counseling groups. This means that I will miss a class period once a week for a total of 15 weeks. In the group sessions, topics covered include trust building, anger management, problem solving, the importance of education for the future, ethnic pride, dealing with discrimination, avoiding peer pressure and gangs, family relationships, and coping with community violence. Specific activities are presented in each session and I will also be encouraged to share my own feelings and experiences.

I will be asked to complete a brief interview now and one after the groups have ended. During the interview, I will be asked to talk about things in my life. I can skip any questions I do not wish to answer, and I can stop the interview at any time. If I am feeling upset at the end of the interview, the interviewer will give me the phone number of a counselor with whom I can talk about problems I may be having.

What I say during the interview and in the SPARK groups will be kept confidential. This means that what I say will not be shared with my parents, teachers, or friends. The SPARK leader will not tell anyone what I say without my permission unless there is something that could be dangerous to me or to someone else. If I indicate that someone is or has been hurting me, the leader will have to tell the people who are responsible for protecting children, so they can make sure that I am safe. If I indicate I am thinking about hurting myself, the leader will have to tell my parents and school counselor in order to keep me safe.

My parents or I can always call the SPARK leader if we have any questions about the groups or the interview. I have read this form, and I understand it.

_____   _____

Student's Signature   **Date**

_____   _____

SPARK Leader   **SPARK Leader's Phone Number**

Pregroup and Postgroup Interview

Student's Name: _____ Ethnicity: _____

Gender: _____ Administered by: _____ Date: _____

Circle One: Pregroup   Postgroup

Section 1: Background Information

Demographics

I'm going to start by asking you some general questions

1. What grade are you in? _____

2. What is your birthdate? _____ So you're _____ years old?

3. Who do you live with? (list) _____

   Does anyone else live in your house with you? (list) _____

List siblings: Brother/sister	Age	Lives with you?
_____	_____	Y/N
_____	_____	Y/N
_____	_____	Y/N

4. So you don't live with (mom, dad, mom or dad)? Why is that? (circle M for mom, D for dad)

Divorce	M	D	Parent in jail	M	D
Separated	M	D	Other (specify) _____		
Death	M	D	Don't know		
Never married	M	D			

5. How often have you moved in your life?

   Never   3–5 times

   Once or twice   More than 5 times

APPENDIX A-5   From Waterman and Walker (2000). Copyright 2000 by The Guilford Press.

Family Stressors

I'm going to read you a list of things that sometimes happen to people your age. For each event, tell me if it has happened to you during the last year. If it has happened during the last year, tell me how stressful it was for you when it occurred. *(Show Response Scale 1.)*

No				Yes				
N	1		2		3		4	
	No trouble		Bothersome		Stressful		Very stressful	

During the last year

1. Did one of your parents start or stop working?	N	1	2	3	4
2. Did your parents separate or get a divorce?	N	1	2	3	4
3. Did you argue more with your parents?	N	1	2	3	4
4. Did your parents argue much more with each other?	N	1	2	3	4
5. Did someone in your family have a problem with drug or alcohol use?	N	1	2	3	4
6. Did someone important to you go to jail or prison?	N	1	2	3	4

Community Violence Exposure

Now I will be asking about various kinds of violence that you may have experienced, seen, or heard about in real life. These questions do not include things that you have seen or heard about only on TV, radio, in the news, or in the movies. For each question, I will be asking if the event happened to you, if you have seen it happen, or if you know someone that it happened to. *(Show Response Scale 2.)*

	Happened to me (a)	Saw it happen (b)	Know someone it happened to (c)	None of these (d)
1. Chased by gangs or individuals	_____	_____	_____	_____
2. Beaten up or mugged	_____	_____	_____	_____
3. Attacked or stabbed with a knife	_____	_____	_____	_____
4. Shot or shot at with a gun	_____	_____	_____	_____

APPENDIX A-5   From Waterman and Walker (2000). Copyright 2000 by The Guilford Press.

5. Someone broke into or tried to force their way into the house or apartment

    _____ a. I have had this happen to me when I was home.

    _____ b. I have had this happen to me when I was not home.

    _____ c. I have seen this happen to someone else's house or apartment.

    _____ d. I know someone who this happened to.

    _____ e. None of the above.

6. Someone carrying or holding a gun or a knife (not including police, military, or security officers)

    _____ a. I have seen this.

    _____ b. I know someone who carries a gun or knife.

    _____ c. None of the above.

7. Gunfire

    _____ a. I was in my home and I saw a gun fired outside or inside of my home.

    _____ b. This has not happened to me.

8. A dead person somewhere in the community (not including wakes or funerals)

    _____ a. I have seen a dead person.

    _____ b. I have heard about someone else seeing a dead person.

    _____ c. None of the above.

9. Killed by another person (either accidentally or intentionally)

    _____ a. I have seen someone being killed.

    _____ b. I know someone who was killed.

    _____ c. None of the above.

10. Drive-by shooting

    _____ a. I was shot at.

    _____ b. I witnessed one.

    _____ c. I participated in one.

    _____ d. None of the above.

11. Have you been exposed to any other kind of violence that we haven't talked about?
    Y   N

    What happened? _____

    _____

Section II: Other Information Relevant to SPARK Groups

Educational Aspirations

Next, I will be asking you some questions about school. *(Show Response Scale 3.)*

1	2	3	4	5
Less likely than almost all other kids	Less likely than many other kids	About as likely as other kids	More likely than many other kids	More likely than almost all other kids

1. Compared to other kids in your school, how likely is it that you will finish high school? _____

2. Compared to other kids in your school, how likely is it that you will go to college? _____

(Show Response Scale 4.)

1	2	3	4	5
Less important than to almost all others	Less important than to others	About as important as to others	More important than to others	More important than to almost all others

3. Compared to other kids in your school, how important is it to you that you do well in your schoolwork? _____

Adjustment

I'm going to read you a list of things that some kids your age experience. Please tell me how often each of these things happens to you. *(Show Response Scale 5.)*

0	1	2	3
Never	Sometimes	Lots of times	Almost all of the time

	0	1	2	3
1. Feeling lonely	0	1	2	3
2. Remembering things you don't want to remember	0	1	2	3
3. Trouble concentrating on things at home or at school	0	1	2	3
4. Wanting to break things	0	1	2	3
5. Wanting to hurt yourself*	0	1	2	3
6. Feeling afraid	0	1	2	3
7. Feeling sad or unhappy	0	1	2	3
8. Can't stop thinking about something bad that happened to you	0	1	2	3
9. Trouble falling asleep or staying asleep	0	1	2	3
10. Wanting to yell at people	0	1	2	3

11. Wanting to kill yourself*	0	1	2	3
12. Trying not to feel anything (bad feelings)	0	1	2	3
13. Worrying about things	0	1	2	3
14. Feeling unlike anybody else	0	1	2	3

*Mark items 5 and 11 for follow-up at end of interview.

Anger Management

Now I'm going to ask you some questions about times when you're angry.

1. In the last month, how many times have you hit, kicked, or slapped someone? _____

2. In the last month, how many times have you been sent to the office for fighting, calling someone a name, arguing with a teacher, etc.? _____

3. In the last month, have you been suspended from school for any reason?   Y   N

   If yes, why?_____

4. You're walking to the store. Someone your age walks up to you and calls you a name. What would you probably do if this happened to you? *(Show Response Scale 6; circle all that apply.)*

A	B	C	D	E
Call him or her a name	**Ask him or her what's going on**	**Walk away from him or her**	**Tell him or her to cut it out**	**Hit him or her**

5. You see your friend fighting with another kid your age. What would you probably do if this happened to you? *(Show Response Scale 7; circle all that apply.)*

A	B	C	D	E
Cheer for your friend to win	**Find out why they are fighting**	**Go away and let them fight it out**	**Try to get them calm down and stop fighthing**	**Join your friend in fighting the other kid**

Self-Esteem

I'm going to read you some statements and I'd like you to tell me how much you agree or disagree with each statement. *(Show Response Scale 8.)*

1	2	3	4
Strongly agree	**Agree**	**Disagree**	**Strongly disagree**

1. I feel that I am a person of worth, at least on an equal basis with others. _____

2. I feel that I have a number of good qualities. _____

3. All in all, I am inclined to feel that I am a failure. _____

4. I am able to do things as well as most other people. _____

5. I feel I do not have much to be proud of. _____

6. I take a positive attitude toward myself. _____

7. On the whole, I am satisfied with myself. _____

8. I wish I could have more respect for myself. _____

9. I certainly feel useless at times. _____

10. At times I think I am no good at all. _____

Ethnic Pride

In a minute I'm going to read you some different statements, but first I'd like to ask you a question. What word would you use to describe your ethnic or racial group? _____ *(If the child has trouble, say, "Martin Luther King might say he is black or African American; Cesar Chavez might say that he is Hispanic or Latino . . .")* **OK, so for these questions, whenever I say "ethnic group" I mean _____. I'd like you to tell me how much you agree or disagree with each statement.** *(Use Response Scale 8 again.)*

1	2	3	4
Strongly agree	**Agree**	**Disagree**	**Strongly disagree**

1. I am happy that I am [*ethnic group from above*]. _____

2. I feel little sense of belonging to my own ethnic group. _____

3. I have a lot of pride in my ethnic group and its accomplishments. _____

4. I feel little attachment towards my own ethnic group. _____

5. I feel good about my cultural or ethnic background. _____

Peer Attachment

These questions ask about your relationships with important people in your life—your close friends. Please tell me how true each statement is for you now. *(Show Response Scale 9.)*

1	2	3	4	5
Almost never, or never true	**Not very often true**	**Sometimes true**	**Often true**	**Almost always or always true**

1. When we discuss things, my friends care about my point of view. _____

2. I feel my friends are good friends. _____

3. I feel angry with my friends. _____

4. I trust my friends. _____

5. My friends help me talk about my difficulties. _____

6. It seems as if my friends are irritated with me for no reason. _____

Gang Involvement

Now, I'm going to ask you some questions about gangs. *(Show Response Scale 10.)*

1	2	3	4	5
None	A few	About half	Most	All or almost all

1. How many of your friends are in a gang? _____

2. How many of your family members are in a gang? _____

(Show Response Scale 11.)

1	2	3	4	5
Not at all necessary	Not very necessary	Somewhat necessary	Pretty necessary	Completely necessary

3. How necessary is it to belong to a gang?_____

   Why do you feel that way? _____

(Show Response Scale 12.)

4. Has anyone ever tried to jump you in a gang?　　Y　　　　N

The interview part is completed. Process any distress responses to items 5 and 11 of the Adjustment scale.

If this is a pregroup interview, say, **"Okay, we're done. Thanks for answering all of these questions. Do you have any questions about any of the things we talked about today? The groups will be starting soon, and they should be a lot of fun."**

If this is a postgroup interview, say, **"Okay, we're done with this part of the interview. I just have one more thing for you to do. I'm going to give you a paper with some questions about the SPARK groups. You don't have to write your name on the paper, so be as honest as possible. When you're done, put your answers in this envelope and seal it so that your answers will be anonymous."** *(Give the student an envelope and the last page of the interview.)*

SPARK Group Evaluation

1	2	3	4	5
Not at all	Just a little	Somewhat	Pretty much	Very much

1. Using the numbers on the response scale above, how much did the SPARK groups help you

    a. Use cool-headed responses when angry? _____

    b. Feel better about yourself? _____

    c. Express your feelings? _____

    d. Resist peer pressure? _____

    e. Feel more accepting of people who are different from you? _____

    f. Understand your reactions to bad things happening to you? _____

    g. Want to do better at school? _____

2. How much did you like the SPARK groups? _____

1	2	3	4	5
Not at all helpful	A little helpful	Somewhat helpful	Pretty helpful	Very helpful

Using the numbers on the response scale above, please answer the following questions:

3. How helpful were the group leaders? _____

4. Overall, how helpful were the SPARK groups? _____

5. What suggestions do you have for improving the SPARK groups?

    _____

    _____

    _____

Thanks for being a member of SPARK!!

Scoring Instructions and Information about the Interview

Some of the measures in the interview were developed specifically for the SPARK program. Whenever possible, however, we used measures that were already in existence and well documented. In some cases, we adapted those measures for the purposes of the SPARK program. Below is a description of the various measures. References for the measures can be found in the References section at the end of the book.

Section I—Background Information

Demographics: The items in this section involve basic information, including grade level, family structure, and living situation.

Family Stressors: This scale includes items drawn from the *Junior High Life Experiences Survey* (Swearingen & Cohen, 1985) that pertain specifically to stress and distress within the immediate family. *Scoring:* "No" responses are scored as 0; total the responses to the 6 items, and divide by 6 to get the mean family stressors score.

Community Violence Exposure: This scale is an adaptation of the self-report version of the *Survey of Children's Exposure to Community Violence* (Richters & Saltzman, 1990). The scale has 3 subscales: Direct, Witness, and Vicarious violence exposure. *Scoring:* "Yes" responses are scored as "1" and "no" responses are scored as 0; total the responses to 1a, 2a, 3a, 4a, 5a, 5b, 10a, and 10c, and divide by 8 to get the mean Direct violence exposure score; total the responses to 1b, 2b, 3b, 4b, 5c, 6a, 7a, 8a, 9a, and 10b, and divide by 10 to get the mean Witness violence exposure score; total the responses to 1c, 2c, 3c, 4c, 5d, 6b, 8b, and 9b, and divide by 8 to get the mean Vicarious violence exposure score.

Section II—Other Information Relevant to SPARK Groups

Educational Aspirations: These items were developed specifically for the SPARK program. *Scoring:* Total the responses to the 3 items, and divide by 3 to get the mean educational aspirations score.

Adjustment: Most of the items from this scale were drawn from the *Trauma Symptom Checklist for Children* (TSCC; Briere, 1996). The TSCC has several subscales, including Depression, Anxiety, Anger, and Posttraumatic Stress Disorder (PTSD). Several additional items were also developed specifically for the SPARK program in order to assess the 3 symptom clusters of PTSD: reexperiencing the traumatic event, avoidant behaviors, and hyperarousal. In this shortened version, we included the 2 items from the Depression, Anxiety, and Anger subscales that had the highest item-scale correlation in our sample. We also included 6 PTSD items—the 2 items from each of the 3 symptom clusters (i.e., reexperiencing, avoidance, and hyperarousal) that had the highest item-scale correlation in our sample. Finally, we included 2 items that assess for suicidality (i.e., wanting to hurt yourself; wanting to kill yourself); these 2 items can be included in the Depression subscale. *Scoring:* Total the responses to items 1, 5, 7, and 11, and divide by 4 to get the mean Depression score; total the responses to items 6 and 13, and divide by 2 to get the mean Anxiety score; total the responses to items 4 and 10, and divide by 2 to

APPENDIX A-6 From Waterman and Walker (2000). Copyright 2000 by The Guilford Press.

get the mean Anger score; total the responses to items 2 and 8, and divide by 2 to get the mean PTSD–reexperiencing score; total the responses to items 12 and 14, and divide by 2 to get the mean PTSD–avoidance score; total the responses to items 3 and 9, and divide by 2 to get the mean PTSD–hyperarousal score; total the responses to items 2, 3, 8, 9, 12, and 14, and divide by 6 to get the mean PTSD score; total the responses to all 14 items, and divide by 14 to get the mean adjustment score.

Anger Management: The first 3 items were developed specifically for the SPARK program. The last 2 items were drawn from a scale developed by Slaby and Wilson-Brewer (1992). *Scoring:* The first 3 items should not be combined to form a total score (i.e., look at each item individually). For items 4 and 5, give a score of 0 if only B, C, and/or D responses are circled; give a score of 1 if A but not E is circled (B, C, and/or D may also be circled); give a score of 2 if E but not A is circled (B, C, and/or D may also be circled); give a score of 3 if both A and E are circled (B, C, and/or D may also be circled); then, total the scores for items 4 and 5 and divide by 2 to get the mean anger management score.

Self-Esteem: This scale is an unmodified version of the *Rosenberg Self-Esteem Scale* (Rosenberg, 1979). *Scoring:* Reverse score items 3, 5, 8, 9, and 10 (e.g., a score of 4 would be a 1, a score of 3 would be a 2, etc.); total the responses to the 10 items, and divide by 10 to get the mean self-esteem score.

Ethnic Pride: These items were adapted from the Affirmation and Belonging subscale of the *Multigroup Ethnic Identity Measure* (Phinney, 1992). *Scoring:* Reverse score items 2 and 4 (e.g., a score of 4 would be a 1, a score of 3 would be a 2, etc.); total the responses to the 5 items, and divide by 5 to get the mean ethnic pride score.

Peer Attachment: These items were drawn from the Peer scale of the *Inventory of Parent and Peer Attachment* (Armsden & Greenberg, 1987). The Peer scale includes 3 subscales: Trust, Communication, and (Lack of) Alienation. In our shortened version of the Peer scale, we included the 2 items from each subscale that had the highest item-scale correlation in our sample. *Scoring:* Reverse score items 3 and 6 (e.g., a score of 5 would be a 1, a score of 4 would be a 2, etc.); total the responses to items 2 and 4, and divide by 2 to get the mean Trust score; total the responses to items 1 and 5, and divide by 2 to get the mean Communication score; total the responses to items 3 and 6, and divide by 2 to get the mean (Lack of) Alienation score; total all 6 items, and divide by 6 to get the mean peer attachment score.

Gang Involvement: The gang involvement items were developed specifically for the SPARK program. *Scoring:* "Yes" responses to item 4 should be scored as 5, and "No" responses scored as 1; total the responses to the 4 items, and divide by 4 to get the mean gang involvement score.

Response Scale 1 for the Interview

Yes		
	Very stressful	4
	Stressful	3
	Bother-some	2
	No trouble	1
No		N

Response Scale 2 for the Interview

A	B	C	D
I have had this happen to *me*	I have seen this happen to *someone else*	I know someone who this happened to	*None of these*

APPENDIX A-7 From Waterman and Walker (2000). Copyright 2000 by The Guilford Press.

Response Scale 3 for the Interview

1	2	3	4	5
Less likely than almost all other kids	Less likely than many other kids	About as likely as other kids	More likely than many other kids	More likely than almost all other kids

APPENDIX A-7   From Waterman and Walker (2000). Copyright 2000 by The Guilford Press.

Response Scale 4 for the Interview

1	2	3	4	5
Less important than to almost all others	Less important than to others	About as important as to others	More important than to others	More important than to almost all others

Response Scale 5 for the Interview

3	2	1	0
Almost all of the time	Lots of times	Sometimes	Never

APPENDIX A-7 From Waterman and Walker (2000). Copyright 2000 by The Guilford Press.

Response Scale 6 for the Interview

A	B	C	D	E
	Ask him or her what's going on	Walk away from him or her	Tell him or her to cut it out	Hit him or her
Call him or her a name				

A	B	C	D	E
Cheer for your friend to win	Find out why they are fighting	Go away and let them fight it out	Try to get them to calm down and stop fighting	Join your friend in fighting the other kid

1	2	3	4
Strongly agree	Agree	Disagree	Strongly disagree

APPENDIX A-7   From Waterman and Walker (2000). Copyright 2000 by The Guilford Press.

Response Scale 9 for the Interview

1	2	3	4	5
Almost never, or never true	Not very often true	Sometimes true	Often true	Almost always, or always true

APPENDIX A-7   From Waterman and Walker (2000). Copyright 2000 by The Guilford Press.

Response Scale 10 for the Interview

1	2	3	4	5
None	A few	About half	Most	All or almost all

Response Scale 11 for the Interview

1	2	3	4	5
Not at all necessary	Not very necessary	Somewhat necessary	Pretty necessary	Completely necessary

Response Scale 12 for the Interview

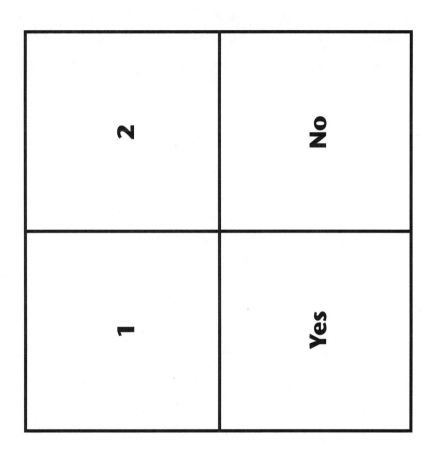

Curriculum Materials and Handouts

Module Six: Exposure to Violence and Posttraumatic Stress Reactions

Termination Session: The Party

Module One: Trust Building and Communication Skills

Session One

1. Trust ratings (Appendix B-1a)

   a. Make enough copies for each student to complete one rating slip.
   b. Cut slips along dotted line.
   c. Ask students to complete these forms at the beginning of the first session.
   d. You may need to bring some trust ratings to Session Two for new members.
   e. Trust ratings for each student are also needed in Session Three of the Trust Building and Communication Skills module and at the Final Session of the groups.

2. Confidentiality Contract (Appendix B-1b)

   a. Make enough copies for each student to complete one contract.
   b. You may need to bring some Confidentiality Contracts to Session Two for students who did not attend Session One or who wanted to think about whether they were willing to sign.

Session Two

1. Feelings for Feelings Grab Bag (Appendix B-1c)

   a. Cut paper to separate individual feelings, and fold in half.
   b. Add other feelings if they seem important for your particular group.
   c. Place the folded feelings in a hat or bag.

Session Three

1. Trust ratings (see Session One)

2. Secrets for Secret Pooling (Low-Trust Version) (Appendix B-1d)

   a. Use prepared secrets if the average of the trust ratings at the beginning of Session Three is less than 3.
   b. Select the younger or older version of secrets as appropriate for the group.
   c. Bring one copy for each group you are running.
   d. Cut paper to separate individual secrets and fold in half.
   e. Place in hat or bag.

3. Helping Responses handout (Appendix B-1e)

   a. Make a copy for each student.

Trust Ratings

Name: _____ Date: _____

How much do you trust the other members of the group?

1	2	3	4	5
Not at all	Just a little	Somewhat	Pretty much	Very much

- -

Name: _____ Date: _____

How much do you trust the other members of the group?

1	2	3	4	5
Not at all	Just a little	Somewhat	Pretty much	Very much

- -

Name: _____ Date: _____

How much do you trust the other members of the group?

1	2	3	4	5
Not at all	Just a little	Somewhat	Pretty much	Very much

- -

Name: _____ Date: _____

How much do you trust the other members of the group?

1	2	3	4	5
Not at all	Just a little	Somewhat	Pretty much	Very much

- -

Name: _____ Date: _____

How much do you trust the other members of the group?

1	2	3	4	5
Not at all	Just a little	Somewhat	Pretty much	Very much

- -

Name: _____ Date: _____

How much do you trust the other members of the group?

1	2	3	4	5
Not at all	Just a little	Somewhat	Pretty much	Very much

- -

Confidentiality Contract

I understand that anything I say or do during the group will not be revealed by the group leaders to anyone outside the group, including my parents, friends, and teachers. I understand that the only exception is if I reveal information about myself or someone else's being in danger; then, the group leader will have to tell someone in order to keep me or someone else safe.

I also understand that I cannot talk to anyone else about what other people say or do in the group. This includes talking to my parents, brothers and sisters, and friends. I understand that the other members of this group will be trusting me with their secrets and that to talk about what they say would be breaking their trust.

By signing this contract, I agree not to talk to anyone outside of the group about what others say or do in the group.

_____   _____

Group Member's Signature   **Date**

Feelings for Feelings Grab Bag

Scared	**Proud**
Shy	**Disappointed**
Brave	**Confused**
Sad	**Happy**
Surprised	**Embarrassed**
Frustrated	**Excited**
Relaxed	**Stressed**
Ashamed	**Confident**

Secrets for Secret Pooling—
Low-Trust Version (Younger Students)

Secret

I am in a gang.

Instructions:
1. **Read this secret out loud as if it were your own secret.**
2. **Say how you would feel if this were your own secret.**

- -

Secret

I have smoked marijuana.

Instructions:
1. **Read this secret out loud as if it were your own secret.**
2. **Say how you would feel if this were your own secret.**

- -

Secret

I have shoplifted.

Instructions:
1. **Read this secret out loud as if it were your own secret.**
2. **Say how you would feel if this were your own secret.**

- -

Secret

I have been held back a grade.

Instructions:
1. **Read this secret out loud as if it were your own secret.**
2. **Say how you would feel if this were your own secret.**

- -

Secret

I have been picked up by the police.

Instructions:
1. **Read this secret out loud as if it were your own secret.**
2. **Say how you would feel if this were your own secret.**

- -

Secret

My parents are getting a divorce.

Instructions:
1. **Read this secret out loud as if it were your own secret.**
2. **Say how you would feel if this were your own secret.**

- -

Secret

I cheat on tests.

Instructions:
1. **Read this secret out loud as if it were your own secret.**
2. **Say how you would feel if this were your own secret.**

- -

Secret

My dad is in jail.

Instructions:
1. **Read this secret out loud as if it were your own secret.**
2. **Say how you would feel if this were your own secret.**

- -

Secret

I have gotten drunk.

Instructions:
1. **Read this secret out loud as if it were your own secret.**
2. **Say how you would feel if this were your own secret.**

- -

Secret

I sometimes feel like killing myself.

Instructions:
1. **Read this secret out loud as if it were your own secret.**
2. **Say how you would feel if this were your own secret.**

- -

Secret

_____

Instructions:
1. **Read this secret out loud as if it were your own secret.**
2. **Say how you would feel if this were your own secret.**

- -

Secret

_____

Instructions:
1. **Read this secret out loud as if it were your own secret.**
2. **Say how you would feel if this were your own secret.**

- -

Secret

_____

Instructions:
1. **Read this secret out loud as if it were your own secret.**
2. **Say how you would feel if this were your own secret.**

- -

Secret

_____

Instructions:
1. **Read this secret out loud as if it were your own secret.**
2. **Say how you would feel if this were your own secret.**

- -

Secret

_____

Instructions:
1. **Read this secret out loud as if it were your own secret.**
2. **Say how you would feel if this were your own secret.**

- -

Secrets for Secret Pooling—
Low-Trust Version (Older Students)

Secret

I am in a gang.

Instructions:
1. Read this secret out loud as if it were your own secret.
2. Say how you would feel if this were your own secret.

- -

Secret

I have smoked marijuana.

Instructions:
1. Read this secret out loud as if it were your own secret.
2. Say how you would feel if this were your own secret.

- -

Secret

I have shoplifted.

Instructions:
1. Read this secret out loud as if it were your own secret.
2. Say how you would feel if this were your own secret.

- -

Secret

Girls: I got pregnant and had an abortion.
OR
Guys: I got my girlfriend pregnant and she had an abortion.

Instructions:
1. Read this secret out loud as if it were your own secret.
2. Say how you would feel if this were your own secret.

- -

Secret

I have been picked up by the police.

Instructions:
1. Read this secret out loud as if it were your own secret.
2. Say how you would feel if this were your own secret.

Secret

My parents are getting a divorce.

Instructions:
1. Read this secret out loud as if it were your own secret.
2. Say how you would feel if this were your own secret.

- -

Secret

I have had sex.

Instructions:
1. Read this secret out loud as if it were your own secret.
2. Say how you would feel if this were your own secret.

- -

Secret

My dad is in jail.

Instructions:
1. Read this secret out loud as if it were your own secret.
2. Say how you would feel if this were your own secret.

- -

Secret

I have gotten drunk.

Instructions:
1. Read this secret out loud as if it were your own secret.
2. Say how you would feel if this were your own secret.

- -

Secret

I sometimes feel like killing myself.

Instructions:
1. Read this secret out loud as if it were your own secret.
2. Say how you would feel if this were your own secret.

- -

Secret

_____

Instructions:

1. **Read this secret out loud as if it were your own secret.**
2. **Say how you would feel if this were your own secret.**

- -

Secret

_____

Instructions:

1. **Read this secret out loud as if it were your own secret.**
2. **Say how you would feel if this were your own secret.**

- -

Secret

_____

Instructions:

1. **Read this secret out loud as if it were your own secret.**
2. **Say how you would feel if this were your own secret.**

- -

Secret

_____

Instructions:

1. **Read this secret out loud as if it were your own secret.**
2. **Say how you would feel if this were your own secret.**

- -

Secret

_____

Instructions:

1. **Read this secret out loud as if it were your own secret.**
2. **Say how you would feel if this were your own secret.**

- -

Helping Responses

Ways to Be Helpful to Someone Who Is Upset or Has a Problem

1. **Listen carefully** to what the person says. Look at the person, and give full attention. Do not interrupt. Try to understand what the person is feeling.

2. **Let the person know you hear and understand their feelings.** Examples are "You must feel really sad about it," "That made you furious," or "That must be so hard for you to deal with."

3. **Share a similar experience** so the person does not feel so alone. Keep the focus on the person with the problem, not on you.

Nonhelpful Ways of Responding

1. **Telling the person what to do.** Do not give advice.

2. **Putting down the person with the problem.** You want to help the person feel accepted, rather than feeling bad about sharing the problem.

3. **Asking lots of questions out of curiosity.** Focus on what is going on with the person rather than on things you want to know.

Module Two: Anger Management and Problem-Solving Skills

Session One

1. Problem-Solving cartoon (Appendix B-2a)

    a. Make one copy for each student.

2. Hot-Head Cool-Head game cards (Appendix B-2b)

    a. Use different color cards or paper for Problems, Alternatives, and Consequences.

    b. Copy statements onto cards, remembering to use both sides.

    c. Cut and, if possible, laminate cards.

3. Cool-Head Responses handout (Appendix B-2c)

    a. Make one copy for each student.

    b. Bring extras for Session Two.

Problem-Solving Cartoon

Hot-Head Cool-Head Game Cards

PROBLEM	**PROBLEM**
PROBLEM	**PROBLEM**
PROBLEM	**PROBLEM**
PROBLEM	**PROBLEM**
PROBLEM	**PROBLEM**
PROBLEM	**PROBLEM**
PROBLEM	**PROBLEM**
PROBLEM	**PROBLEM**

My brother or sister was bothering me.	**My mom or dad punished me for no reason.**
Another kid was picking on my friend.	**Another kid took something that belonged to me.**
My boyfriend/girlfriend went out with somebody else.	**Somebody cheated so that they would beat me.**
Another kid said something about my mother.	**My teacher was picking on me.**
Somebody made a racist comment to me.	**Another kid pushed me.**
Another kid stole money from me.	**I got blamed for something I did not do.**
My friend told someone a secret of mine.	**Another kid called me really bad names.**
My best friend went out with my girlfriend/boyfriend.	**My brother took money from me.**

ALTERNATIVE	**ALTERNATIVE**
ALTERNATIVE	**ALTERNATIVE**
ALTERNATIVE	**ALTERNATIVE**
ALTERNATIVE	**ALTERNATIVE**
ALTERNATIVE	**ALTERNATIVE**
ALTERNATIVE	**ALTERNATIVE**
ALTERNATIVE	**ALTERNATIVE**
ALTERNATIVE	**ALTERNATIVE**

✷✷✷HOT✷✷✷	✷✷✷HOT✷✷✷
✷✷✷HOT✷✷✷	✷✷✷HOT✷✷✷
✷✷✷HOT✷✷✷	✷✷✷HOT✷✷✷
✷✷✷HOT✷✷✷	✷✷✷HOT✷✷✷
❄❄❄COOL❄❄❄	❄❄❄COOL❄❄❄
❄❄❄COOL❄❄❄	❄❄❄COOL❄❄❄
❄❄❄COOL❄❄❄	❄❄❄COOL❄❄❄
❄❄❄COOL❄❄❄	❄❄❄COOL❄❄❄

140

CONSEQUENCE	CONSEQUENCE
CONSEQUENCE	CONSEQUENCE
CONSEQUENCE	CONSEQUENCE
CONSEQUENCE	CONSEQUENCE
CONSEQUENCE	CONSEQUENCE
CONSEQUENCE	CONSEQUENCE
CONSEQUENCE	CONSEQUENCE
CONSEQUENCE	CONSEQUENCE

SHORT-TERM FOR YOU	**LONG-TERM FOR YOU**
SHORT-TERM FOR YOU	**LONG-TERM FOR YOU**
SHORT-TERM FOR YOU	**LONG-TERM FOR YOU**
SHORT-TERM FOR YOU	**LONG-TERM FOR YOU**
SHORT-TERM FOR OTHERS	**LONG-TERM FOR OTHERS**
SHORT-TERM FOR OTHERS	**LONG-TERM FOR OTHERS**
SHORT-TERM FOR OTHERS	**LONG-TERM FOR OTHERS**
SHORT-TERM FOR OTHERS	**LONG-TERM FOR OTHERS**

Cool-Head Responses

During the next week, notice two situations where you get angry.

Use cool-head responses to deal with these situations.

Write them down below, or come prepared to talk about them next week.

If you used a hot-head response, write it down and give a possible cool-head response as well.

I was angry when:

_____

_____

The cool-head response I used was:

_____

_____

I was angry when:

_____

_____

The cool-head response I used was:

_____

_____

I used a hot-head response when:

_____

_____

The cool-head response I could have used was:

_____

_____

Name: _____

Module Three: Ethnic Identity and Anti-Prejudice

Session One

1. Labels for Labeling game (Appendix B-3)

   a. Copy one adjective onto each label with an adhesive backing.

   b. Use different labels if they are more appropriate for your particular group.

   c. Make one label for each student.

   d. Make one set of labels for each group.

Labels for Labeling Game

GOOD STUDENT	**BOSSY**
LAZY	**TEACHER'S PET**
FRIENDLY	**GOOD ATHLETE**
SHY	**SNOBBY**
SEXY	**HELPFUL**
ANGRY	**LONER**
PLAYER	**BIG MOUTH**

Module Four: Educational Aspirations

Session One

1. Education and Career Ladder (Appendix B-4a)

   a. Make one copy for each student.

2. My Goals handout (Appendix B-4b)

   a. Make one copy for each student.

   b. Bring extra goal sheets to Session Three since some students may not remember to bring them back.

Session Three

1. My Goals handout (Appendix B-4b)

   a. Make one copy for each student since some students may not remember to bring back the sheets given out in Session One.

Education and Career Ladder

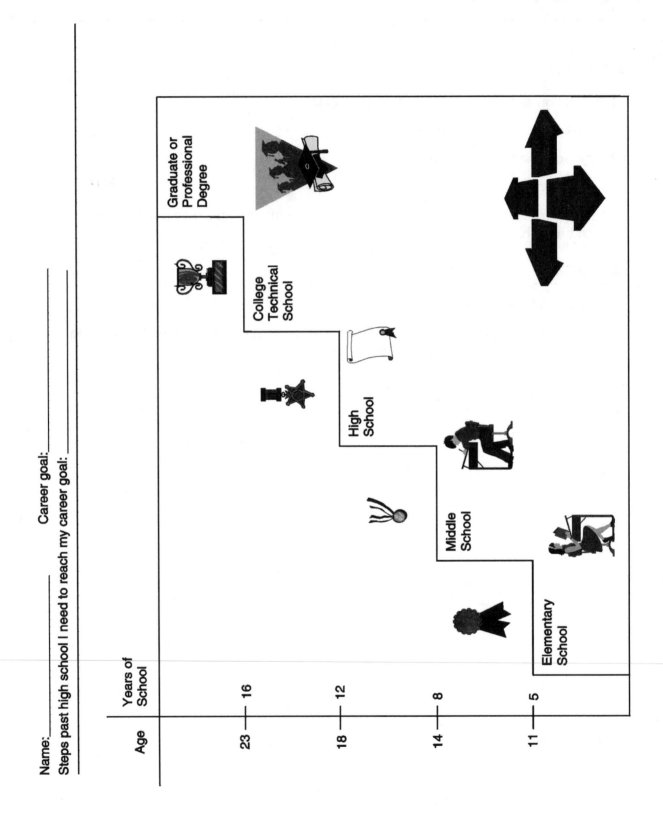

Name: _____

Career goal: _____

Steps past high school I need to reach my career goal: _____

Years of School

Age	Years of School
23	16
18	12
14	8
11	5

Graduate or Professional Degree

College Technical School

High School

Middle School

Elementary School

APPENDIX B-4a   From Waterman and Walker (2000). Copyright 2000 by The Guilford Press.

 # My Goals

I set goals for myself and work toward those goals.

My goals for this school year are:

1. _____

_____

2. _____

_____

3. _____

_____

To achieve these goals, I will:

1. _____

_____

2. _____

_____

3. _____

_____

_____   _____

Signature   **Date**

Module Five: Peer Pressure and Gangs

Session One

Resisting Peer Pressure handout (Appendix B-5)

Make one copy for each student.

Resisting Peer Pressure

Situation where I was pressured:

_____

_____

_____

| **I resisted!!!!!!** | **I gave in . . .** |
| **Strategies I used:** | **The reason is:** |

_____	_____
_____	_____
_____	_____
_____	_____

Situation where I was pressured:

_____

_____

_____

| **I resisted!!!!!!** | **I gave in . . .** |
| **Strategies I used:** | **The reason is:** |

_____	_____
_____	_____
_____	_____
_____	_____

Name: _____

Module Six: Exposure to Violence and Posttraumatic Stress Reactions

Session Two

1. Posttraumatic Stress Reactions handout (Appendix B-6a)

   a. Make one copy for each student.

2. Round disks for posttraumatic stress reactions (Appendix B-6b)

   a. Make 50 disks for each of the three categories.

   b. Use different-colored paper for each of the three categories; suggested colors: green for "reexperiencing," orange for "avoiding," purple for "edge," but feel free to be creative.

Posttraumatic Stress Reactions

- Happens after a very frightening event.

- Very common in students who have been exposed to violence at home, at school, or in the neighborhood.

- Can happen if you are the victim of violence or if you see the violence.

- Are *normal* reactions to *abnormal* situations.

- Three types of reactions:

  1. *Reexperiencing the trauma.*

     a. Memories or thoughts of the trauma suddenly popping into your mind.

     b. Dreaming about what happened over and over.

     c. Feeling that the traumatic event is happening again, like flashbacks.

     d. Getting really nervous or uncomfortable if you go near where it happened.

  2. *Avoiding the trauma.*

     a. Avoiding people, places, or activities that remind you of the trauma.

     b. Feeling cut off from other people or numb, where you don't feel anything.

     c. Being less interested in things you liked to do before the trauma.

     d. Thinking you won't have a career or a family or that you will die young.

  3. *Feeling more on edge.*

     a. Having trouble falling asleep or staying asleep.

     b. Being irritable or getting angry really easily.

     c. Getting distracted and having trouble paying attention.

     d. Being super-aware of where danger might be or startling really easily.

Disks for Posttraumatic Stress Reactions

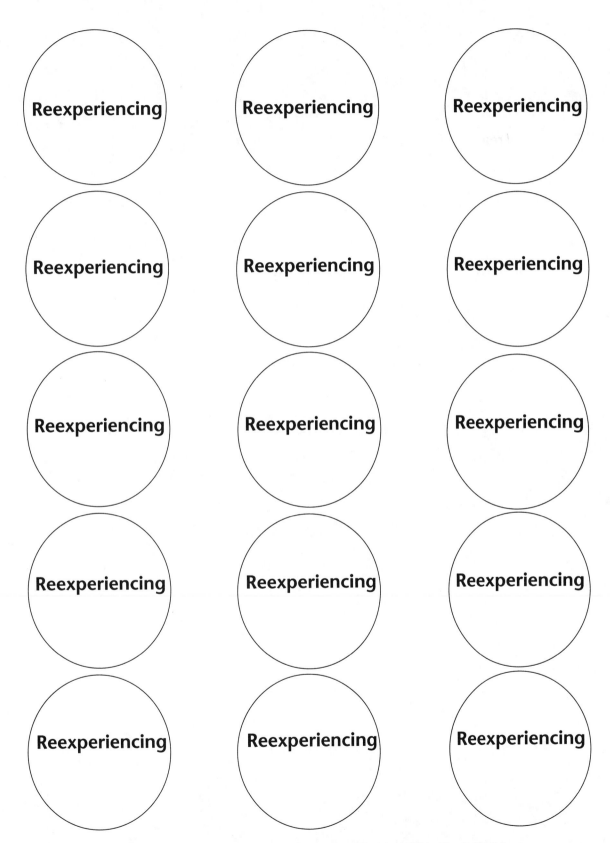

Reexperiencing

Reexperiencing

Reexperiencing

Reexperiencing

Reexperiencing

Reexperiencing

Reexperiencing

Reexperiencing

Reexperiencing

Reexperiencing

Reexperiencing

Reexperiencing

Reexperiencing

Reexperiencing

Reexperiencing

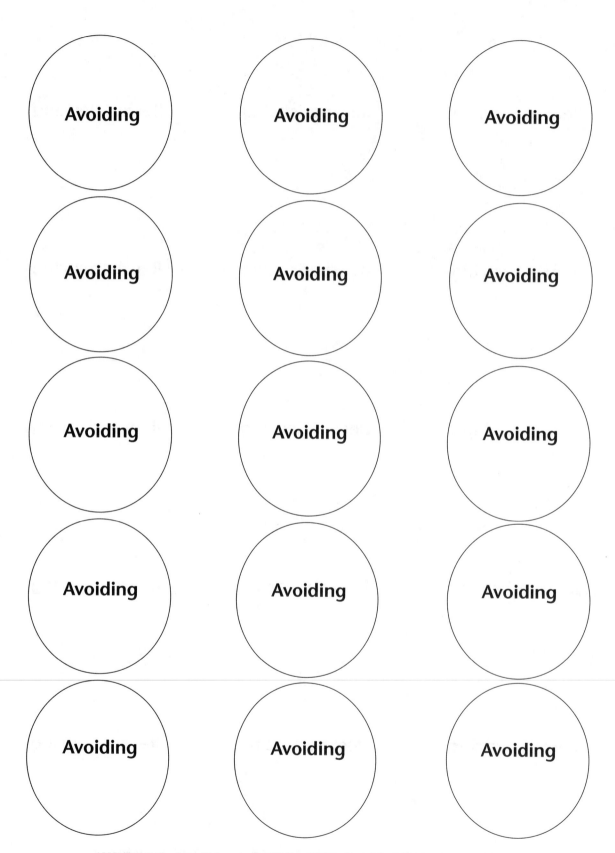

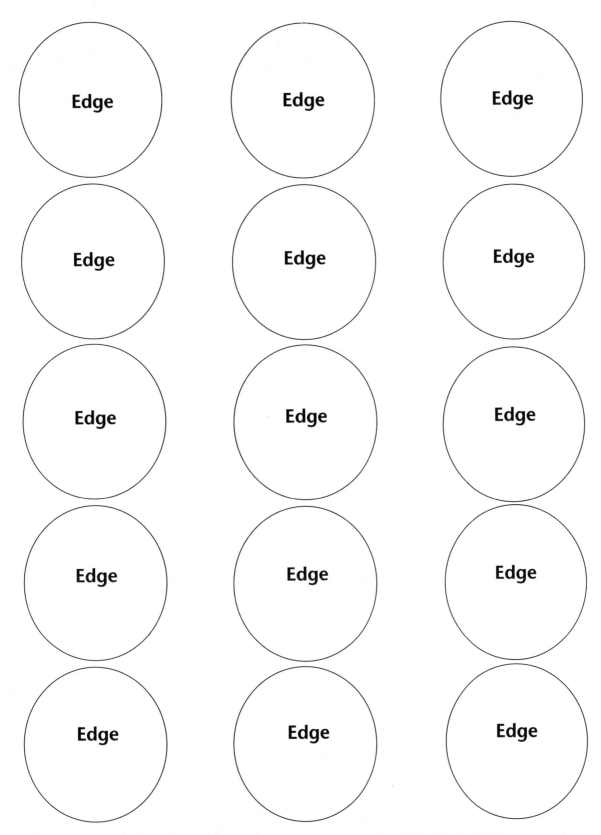

APPENDIX B-6b   From Waterman and Walker (2000). Copyright 2000 by The Guilford Press.

Termination Session: The Party

1. What I Like about You sheet (Appendix B-7a)

   a. Copy on colored paper.

   b. Bring one sheet for each student.

   c. Write down what is said when group members share something they like about each member.

2. Certificate (Appendix B-7b)

   a. Bring one for each student.

   b. Fill out the information (e.g., student's name) before the beginning of the last session.

What I Like about You

Name: _____

Group Member   **What I like about you is . . .**

_____   _____

                                         _____

_____   _____

                                         _____

_____   _____

                                         _____

_____   _____

                                         _____

_____   _____

                                         _____

_____   _____

                                         _____

_____   _____

                                         _____

_____   _____

                                         _____

_____   _____

                                         _____

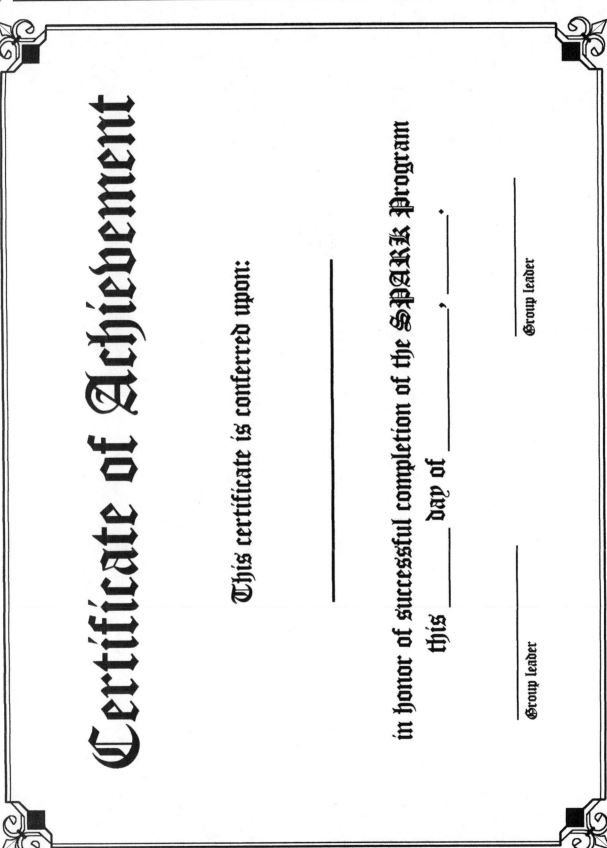

Certificate of Achievement

This certificate is conferred upon:

_____

in honor of successful completion of the SPARK Program

this _____ day of _____, _____.

_____
Group leader

_____
Group leader

Sample Materials in Spanish for Beginning SPARK Groups

Permission to photocopy the forms in this appendix is granted to purchasers of this book for personal use only (see copyright page for details).

Consentimiento de Padres para Participar en SPARK

¿Qué Son los Grupos SPARK?

Los grupos de consejería SPARK son para estudiantes que han sido identificados por un consejero escolar o algún maestro como estudiantes con el potencial de trabajar cooperativamente en un grupo y quienes podrían beneficiarse de este tipo de experiencia. Para participar en los grupos de SPARK, los estudiantes perderán un período de clase una vez a la semana por un total de 15 semanas. En las sesiones de grupo se cubrirán los siguientes tópicos: desarrollo de confianza, manejo del enojo, resolución de conflictos, la importancia de la educación para el futuro, orgullo étnico o racial, cómo enfrentar la discriminación, cómo evitar la presión de grupo y las pandillas, las relaciones familiares, y cómo enfrentar la violencia en la comunidad. Actividades específicas serán presentadas en cada sesión y se le pedirá a los estudiantes que compartan sus propios sentimientos y experiencias.

Los estudiantes serán entrevistados antes y después de participar en los grupos. La entrevista contiene preguntas sobre los sentimientos, actitudes, creencias, experiencias, tensiones y comportamientos problemáticos de los estudiantes.

Confidencialidad

Las respuestas de los estudiantes a las preguntas de la entrevista y su participación en los grupos SPARK serán confidenciales, excepto lo requerido por ley. El privilegio de confidencialidad no se extiende a información sobre abuso sexual, emocional, o físico, o negligencia del un niño. Si el líder de SPARK tiene sospecha razonable o recibe tal información, es deber del líder reportarlo a las autoridades. También, si el líder de SPARK cree que un estudiante de SPARK está en riesgo de hacerse daño a sí mismo o a sí misma o a otra persona, el líder tendrá que mantener la seguridad del estudiante informando al padre o guardián y al consejero de la escuela.

Participación y Retiro

Participación en la entrevista y en los grupos de SPARK es voluntaria. Si un estudiante no participa, no habra consecuencias negativas en la relación con la escuela o en el salón de clase. Puede contactar a el líder de SPARK al teléfono al fondo si tiene preguntas o preocupaciones sobre la entrevista o los grupos.

Doy permiso para que mi hijo/a participe en los grupos de SPARK, tal como están descritos aquí. Al firmar este formulario, doy reconocimiento de que he recibido una copia del formulario de consentimiento.

Firma del Padre y Fecha   **Nombre del Estudiante**

Líder de SPARK   **Teléfono del Líder de SPARK**

Consentimiento del Estudiante para Participar en SPARK

Estoy invitado a participar en los grupos de consejería SPARK. Esto significa que faltaré un periodo de clase una vez por semana por un total de 15 semanas. En las sesiones de grupo, los temas de los que se hablará incluyen: establecimiento de confianza, manejo del enojo, resolución de conflictos, la importancia de la educación para el futuro, orgullo étnico o racial, cómo enfrentar la discriminación, cómo evitar la presión de grupo y las pandillas, las relaciones familiares, y cómo enfrentar la violencia comunitaria. Actividades específicas son presentadas en cada sesión y se motiva y facilita que los estudiantes compartan sus propios sentimientos y experiencias.

Se me pedirá que sea parte de una breve entrevista ahora y otra al terminarse los grupos. Durante la entrevista, se me pedirá que hable de aspectos de mi vida. Puedo no responder cualquier pregunta que yo no desea responder y puedo parar la entrevista en cualquier momento. Si me siento mal al final de la entrevista, el entrevistador me dará el teléfono de un consejero con el que pueda platicar acerca de cualquier problema que yo pudiera tener.

Lo que diga durante la entrevista y en los grupos de SPARK será confidencial. Esto quiere decir que lo que yo diga no será compartido con mis padres, maestros(as), o amigos(as). Los líderes de SPARK no le dirán a nadie lo que les diga sin mi permiso a menos de que sea algo peligroso para mí o para otra persona. Si les digo que alguien me esta lastimando o me ha lastimado, el líder tendrá que decirle a las personas que son responsables de proteger a los niños y adolescentes para asegurarse que no estoy en peligro. Si les digo que estoy pensando en hacerme daño, le tendrán que decir a mis padres y al consejero de la escuela para que me mantenga fuera de peligro.

Mis padres y yo podemos llamar al líder de SPARK si tenemos alguna pregunta acerca de los grupos de consejería o de la entrevista. He leído este documento y lo entiendo.

_____
Firma del Estudiante

_____
Fecha

_____
Líder de SPARK

_____
Teléfono del Líder de SPARK

Pregroup and Postgroup Interview: Spanish Version

Student's Name: _____ Ethnicity: _____

Gender: _____ Administered by: _____ Date: _____

Circle One:　　Pregroup　　　　　　Postgroup

Section I: Background Information

Demographics

Voy a empezar por hacerte unas preguntas.

1. ¿En qué año/grado estas? _____

2. ¿Cual es tu fecha de nacimiento? Así que tienes _____ años?

3. ¿Con quién vives? (list) _____

　　¿Hay alguien más que vive en tu casa contigo? (list) _____

List siblings:　Hermano/hermana	Edad	¿Vive contigo?
_____	_____	S/N
_____	_____	S/N
_____	_____	S/N

4. ¿Así que no vives con tu (mamá, papá, mamá y papá)? ¿Por qué?

Divorcio	M	P	Padre/madre en la carcel	M	P
Separados	M	P	Otra razón (specify) _____		
Muerte	M	P	No sé		
Nunca se casaron	M	P			

5. ¿Cuántas veces te has cambiado de casa en toda tu vida?

　　Nunca　　　　　　　3 a 5 veces

　　Una o dos veces　　Más de 5 veces

6. ¿De dónde eres? _____

7. ¿Hace cuánto que vives en los Estados Unidos? _____ años, _____ meses

8. ¿Hace cuánto que viven en los Estados Unidos tus papás? _____ años, _____ meses

9. ¿Qué idioma se habla en tu casa? _____

10. ¿Qué idioma hablas con tus amigos? _____

Family Stressors

Te voy a leer una lista de cosas que algunas veces les pasan a la gente de tu edad. Para cada una de estas cosas, dime si te han pasado durante este ultimo año. En caso de que sí te haya pasado algo este ultimo año, quiero que me digas qué tan difícil fue para ti cuando esto pasó. *(Show Response Scale 1.)*

NO		SI		
N	**1** **Ningún problema**	**2** **Me molestó** **dificultades**	**3** **Me causó** **dificultades**	**4** **Me causó muchas** **dificultades**

Durante este ultimo año.

	N	1	2	3	4
1. Uno de mis papás empezó a trabajar o dejó de trabajar.	N	1	2	3	4
2. Mis papás se separaron o divorciaron.	N	1	2	3	4
3. Me peleé más de lo normal con mis papás.	N	1	2	3	4
4. Mis papás se pelearon mucho más de lo normal entre ellos.	N	1	2	3	4
5. Alguien en mi familia tuvo problemas con drogas o con alcohol.	N	1	2	3	4
6. Alguien importante para mí fue a la carcel.	N	1	2	3	4

Community Violence Exposure

A continuación encontrarás una lista de diversos tipos de actos de violencia que quizás hayas vivido o visto, o que sabes que le han sucedido a alguien en la vida real. Por favor marca la respuesta o las respuestas que sean ciertas para ti. *No incluyas en tus respuestas cosas que hayas visto u oido solo en peliculas, la tele, el radio o en las noticias.* **Algunas preguntas podrán parecerte incómodas, y no tienes que contestarlas. Recuerda que éste es un cuestionario confidencial; nadie sabrá que estas son tus respuestas, ni tus papás, ni tus amigos, ni tus maestros. Marca** *todas* **las respuestas que sean ciertas para ti. Si no lo has vivido, o si no has visto que le pase a alguien, o si no conoces a nadie a quien le haya pasado, entonces marca la respuesta que dice Ninguna de éstas.** *(Show Response Scale 2.)*

	Esto me pasó a mí (a)	He visto cómo le pasó esto a alguien (b)	Conozco a alguien a quien le pasó esto (c)	Ninguna de estas (d)
1. Haber sido perseguido por pandilleros o por desconocidos	_____	_____	_____	_____

2. Haber sido golpeado
   o haber sido víctima
   de un robo   _____ _____ _____ _____

3. Haber sido apuñalado
   o asaltado con
   un cuchillo   _____ _____ _____ _____

4. Haber sido balaceado,
   o herido por
   un balazo   _____ _____ _____ _____

5. Alguien ha entro, o ha tratado de entrar, a robar la casa o el departamento.

   _____ a. Estaba en casa, cuando esto me pasó a mí.

   _____ b. Estaba fuera de la casa cuando esto me pasó a mí.

   _____ c. He visto cómo pasó esto en una casa ajena.

   _____ d. Concozco a alguien a quien le pasó esto.

   _____ e. Ninguna de éstas.

6. Haber visto a alguien armado con pistola o cuchillo (fuera de policías, soldados o guardias).

   _____ a. He visto esto.

   _____ b. Conozco a alguien que lleva pistola o cuchillo.

   _____ c. Ninguna de éstas.

7. Haber oído o visto disparos.

   _____ a. Mientras estaba en mi casa, he visto u oído una pistola disparar fuera
           o dentro de mí casa.

   _____ b. Esto no me ha pasado.

8. Haber visto a alguien muerto en mi barrio (fuera de velorios, entierros o funerales).

   _____ a. He visto a alguien muerto.

   _____ b. He oído de alguien que vió a alguien muerto.

   _____ c. Ninguna de éstas.

9. Haber visto a alguien que murió ya sea por accidente o que fue asesinado.

   _____ a. He visto morir a alguien así.

   _____ b. Conozco a alguien que murió así.

   _____ c. Ninguna de éstas.

10. Disparos o balazos desde un coche.

_____ a. Me han disparado a mí.

_____ b. He visto esto.

_____ c. He participado en esto.

_____ d. Ninguna de éstas.

11. ¿Has estado expuesto algun otro tipo de violencia del cual no hemos hablado?
S   N

¿Qué pasó? _____

_____

SECTION II: Other Information Relevant to SPARK Groups

Educational Aspirations

Ahora te voy hacer unas preguntas acerca de la esculea. *(Show Response Scale 3.)*

1	2	3	4	5
Casi imposible	No muy probable	Igual de probable	Más o menos probable	Muy probable

1. ¿Comparado a otros niños en tu escuela, qué tan probable es que termines high school? _____

2. ¿Comparado a otros niños en tu escuela, qué tan probable es que vayas a la universidad? _____

(Show Response Scale 4.)

1	2	3	4	5
Menos importante que a casi todos	Menos importante que a otros	Casi lo mismo que a otros	Más importante que a otros	Más importante que a casi todos

3. ¿Comparado a otros niños en tu escuela, para ti, que tan importante es que te vaya bien en tus tareas? _____

Adjustment

Te voy a leer algunas cosas que les pasan a algunos muchachos de tu edad. Por favor dime, ¿qué tan seguido te ha pasado cada una de estas cosas? *(Show Response Scale 5.)*

0	1	2	3
Nunca	Algunas veces	Muchas veces	Casi siempre

1. Sentirte solo	0	1	2	3
2. Recordar cosas que no quieres recordar	0	1	2	3
3. Tener dificultad para concentrarte en la escuela o en casa	0	1	2	3

4. Querer gritar y romper cosas	0	1	2	3
5. Querer lastimarte a ti mismo*	0	1	2	3
6. Tener miedo	0	1	2	3
7. Sentirte triste o desconsolado	0	1	2	3
8. No poder dejar de pensar en cosas malas que te pasaron	0	1	2	3
9. Tener dificultad para dormir	0	1	2	3
10. Querer gritarle a la gente	0	1	2	3
11. Querer matarte*	0	1	2	3
12. Tratar de no sentir nada	0	1	2	3
13. Preocuparte de cosas	0	1	2	3
14. Sentirte diferente de todos	0	1	2	3

* Mark items 5 and 11 for follow-up at end of interview.

Anger Management

Te voy hacer unas preguntas acerca de las veces que estas enojadola.

1. ¿En el último mes, cuantas veces le has pegado, pateado, o cacheteado a una persona? _____

2. ¿En el último mes, cuantas veces te han mandado a la oficina por estar peleando, llamandole de un nombre desagradable a alguien, discutiento con tus maestros, etc.? _____

3. ¿En el último mes, te han suspendido de la escuela por alguna razón?   S   N

   ¿Por qué? _____

4. Estás caminando hacia una tienda. Alguien de tu edad se te acerca y te insulta. ¿Qué harías si esto te pasaría a ti? (*Show Response Scale 6;* circle all that apply.)

A	B	C	D	E
Lo insultas	Le preguntas que está pasando	Te alejas de él o ella	Le dices que deje de insultarte	Le pegas

5. Ves a tu amigo/a peleándose con otro/a chico/a de tu edad. ¿Qué harías si esto te pasaría a ti? (*Show Response Scale 7;* check all that apply.)

A	B	C	D	E
Animar a tu amigo/a para que gane	Averiguar por qué están peleando	Alejarme y dejar que se peleen	Tratar de que se calmen y dejen de pelear	Unirme a mi amigo/a en su pelea con la otra persona

Self-Esteem

Te voy a leer algunas frases y quiero que me digas si estás de acuerdo o no con cada cosa que leo. Usa la escala de respuestas para contestar. *(Show Response Scale 8.)*

1	2	3	4
Esto es cierto para mí	Más o menos cierto	Más o menos falso	Esto es falso para mi

1. Creo que soy una persona valiosa, por lo menos igual de valiosa que los demas. _____

2. Creo que tengo bastantes cualidades buenas. _____

3. En general, estoy dispuesto a pensar que soy un fracaso. _____

4. Puedo hacer las cosas tan bien como la demás gente. _____

5. Siento que no tengo mucho de qué sentirme orgulloso. _____

6. Tengo una buena actitud hacia mí mismo. _____

7. En general, estoy satisfecho con mí mismo. _____

8. Me gustaría respetarme mas. _____

9. Me siento inútil algunas veces. _____

10. A veces pienso que no soy buenola para nada. _____

Ethnic Pride

En un minuto te voy a leer unas frases diferentes pero primero quiero hacerte una pregunta. ¿Qué palabra usarías para describir tu grupo étnico o grupo racial?
_____ *(If subject has trouble, say, "Martin Luther King es Negro o Afro-Americano, Cesar Chavez es Hispano o Latino.")* **Bueno, entonces para estas frases, cada vez que diga "grupo étnico" lo que quiero decir es _____ . Unas de las frases a lo mejor no van a ser muy claras, asi que puedes preguntarme si no estas seguro(a) de lo que estoy diciendo. Para estas frases me gustaría que me digas cuánto estas de acuerdo o no de acuerdo con cada una.** *(Use Response Scale 8 again.)*

1	2	3	4
Esto es cierto para mí	Más o menos cierto	Más o menos falso	Esto es falso para mí

1. Estoy contento(a) que soy (ethnic group from above) _____

2. No me siento miembro(a) de mi grupo étnico/racial. _____

3. Me siento muy orgulloso(a) de mi grupo étnico/racial y todo lo que mi grupo ha logrado.

4. No me siento muy unido(a) a mi grupo étnico/racial. _____

5. Me siento bien hacia mi cultura o raíces étnicas. _____

Peer Attachment

Te voy a leer preguntas sobre tus relaciones con gente importante en tu vida—tus amistades cercanas. Estas oraciones que siguen hablan sobre tus sentimientos con respecto a tus amistades cercanas. Por favor dime cuán cierta es cada frase para ti en estos momentos. *(Show Response Scale 9.)*

1	2	3	4	5
Casi nunca o nunca es cierto	No es muy cierto	A veces es cierto	A menudo es cierto	Casi siempre o siempre es cierto

1. Cuando hablamos, a mis amistades les importa mi punto de vista. _____

2. Siento que mis amigos son buenos amigos _____

3. Estoy molesto con mis amistades. _____

4. Confío en mis amigos. _____

5. Mis amigos me ayudan a hablar sobre mis dificultades. _____

6. Parece como si mis amigos estuvieran enojados conmigo sin ninguna razón. _____

Gang Involvement

Ahora te voy hacer preguntas acerca de las pandillas. *(Show Response Scale 10.)*

1	2	3	4	5
Ninguno	Unos pocos	La mitad	Más de la mitad	Todos o casi todos

1. ¿Cuántos de tus amigos(as) son miembros de una pandilla? _____

2. ¿Cuántos miembros de tu familia estan en una pandilla? _____

(Show Response Scale 11.)

1	2	3	4	5
No es nada necesario	No muy necesario	Algo necesario	Muy necesario	Completamente necesario

3. ¿Qué tan necesario es ser miembro(a) de una pandilla? _____

¿Por qué (o por qué no)? _____

(Show Response Scale 12.)

4. ¿Alguien ha intentado golpearte para meterte en una pandilla? Sí   No

Bueno, ya terminamos con la entrevista. ***Don't forget to process any distress responses to items 5 and 11 of the Adjustment scale.***

If this is a pregroup interview, say **"Ya terminamos. Gracias por contestar todas estas preguntas. ¿Tiénes alguna pregunta sobre cualquier cosa que hemos discutido ahora? Los grupos van a comenzar pronto y serán muy divertidos."**

If this is a postgroup interview, say **"Ya terminamos con esta parte de la entrevista. Solo tengo una cosa más para ti. Te voy a dar un papel con algunas preguntas sobre los grupos de SPARK. No tienes que poner tu nombre en el papel, así que puedes ser lo más honesto/a posible. Cuando termines, pon tus respuestas en este sobre y séllalo para que tus respuestas sean anónimas."** *(Give the student an envelope and the last page of the interview.)*

Evaluación de los Grupos de SPARK

1	2	3	4	5
Nada	Un poquito	Algo	Bastante	Mucho

1. Usando los números en la escala de respuestas arriba, ¿cuánto te ayudó el grupo de SPARK para

   a. Usar respuestas frías (cool-headed) cuando te enojas? _____

   b. Sentirte mejor hacia ti mismo/a? _____

   c. Expresar tus sentimientos? _____

   d. Resistir la presión de grupo? _____

   e. Sentir que aceptas más a la gente que es diferente a ti? _____

   f. Comprender tus reacciones a cosas malas que te pasan? _____

   g. Querer salir mejor en la escuela? _____

2. ¿Cuánto te gustó el grupo de SPARK? _____

1	2	3	4	5
Ninguna ayuda	Un poquito de ayuda	Algo de ayuda	Bastante ayuda	Mucha ayuda

Usando los números en la escala de arriba, por favor contesta las siguientes preguntas:

3. ¿Cuánta ayuda te brindaron los líderes del grupo? _____

4. En general, ¿cuánta ayuda te brindó el grupo de SPARK? _____

5. ¿Qué sugerencias tienes para mejorar los grupos de SPARK?

   _____

   _____

   _____

¡¡Gracias por ser un miembro de SPARK!!

Response Scale 1 for the Interview: Spanish Version

Sí			No
	Me causó muchas dificultades		
	Me causó dificultades		
	Me molestó dificultades		
	Ningún problema		
	4	3	2	1	N

Response Scale 2 for the Interview: Spanish Version

d	c	b	a
Ninguna de estas	Conozco a alguien a quien le pasó esto	He visto cómo le pasó esto a alguien	Esto me pasó a mí

Response Scale 3 for the Interview: Spanish Version

1	2	3	4	5
Casi imposible	No muy probable	Igual de probable	Más o menos probable	Muy probable

APPENDIX C-4   From Waterman and Walker (2000). Copyright 2000 by The Guilford Press.

Response Scale 4 for the Interview: Spanish Version

1	2	3	4	5
Menos importante que a casi todos	Menos importante que a otros	Casi lo mismo que a otros	Más importante que a otros	Más importante que a casi todos

APPENDIX C-4   From Waterman and Walker (2000). Copyright 2000 by The Guilford Press.

Response Scale 5 for the Interview: Spanish Version

3	2	1	0
Casi siempre	Muchas veces	Algunas veces	Nunca

APPENDIX C-4   From Waterman and Walker (2000). Copyright 2000 by The Guilford Press.

Response Scale 6 for the Interview: Spanish Version

A	B	C	D	E
Lo insultas	Le preguntas que está pasando	Te alejas de él o ella	Le dices que deje de insultarte	Le pegas

APPENDIX C-4   From Waterman and Walker (2000). Copyright 2000 by The Guilford Press.

Response Scale 7 for the Interview: Spanish Version

A	B	C	D	E
Animar a tu amigo/a para que gane	Averiguar por qué están peleando	Alejarme y dejar que se peleen	Tratar de que se calmen y dejen de pelear	Unirme a mi amigo/a en su pelea con la otra persona

APPENDIX C-4   From Waterman and Walker (2000). Copyright 2000 by The Guilford Press.

Response Scale 8 for the Interview: Spanish Version

1	2	3	4
Esto es cierto para mí	Más o menos cierto	Más o menos falso	Esto es falso para mí

Response Scale 9 for the Interview: Spanish Version

1	2	3	4	5
Casi nunca o nunca es cierto	No es muy cierto	A veces es cierto	A menudo es cierto	Casi siempre o siempre es cierto

Response Scale 10 for the Interview: Spanish Version

1	2	3	4	5
Ninguno	Unos pocos	La mitad	Más de la mitad	Todos o casi todos

Response Scale 11 for the Interview: Spanish Version

1	2	3	4	5
No es nada necesario	No muy necesario	Algo necesario	Muy necesario	Completa-mente necesario

Response Scale 12 for the Interview: Spanish Version

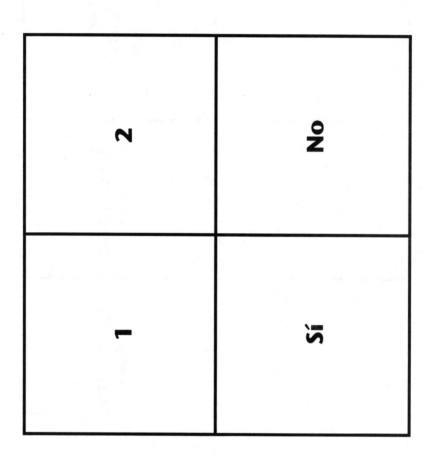

1	2
Sí	No

Curriculum Materials and Handouts in Spanish

Please refer to the corresponding material in Appendix B for detailed instructions.

Module Five: Peer Pressure and Gangs

Module Six: Exposure to Violence and Posttraumatic Stress Reactions

Termination Session: The Party

Trust Ratings: Spanish Version

Nombre: _____ Fecha: _____

¿Cuánto confías en los otros miembros del grupo?

1	2	3	4	5
Nada	Sólo un poco	Algo	Bastante	Mucho

- -

Nombre: _____ Fecha: _____

¿Cuánto confías en los otros miembros del grupo?

1	2	3	4	5
Nada	Sólo un poco	Algo	Bastante	Mucho

- -

Nombre: _____ Fecha: _____

¿Cuánto confías en los otros miembros del grupo?

1	2	3	4	5
Nada	Sólo un poco	Algo	Bastante	Mucho

- -

Nombre: _____ Fecha: _____

¿Cuánto confías en los otros miembros del grupo?

1	2	3	4	5
Nada	Sólo un poco	Algo	Bastante	Mucho

- -

Nombre: _____ Fecha: _____

¿Cuánto confías en los otros miembros del grupo?

1	2	3	4	5
Nada	Sólo un poco	Algo	Bastante	Mucho

- -

Nombre: _____ Fecha: _____

¿Cuánto confías en los otros miembros del grupo?

1	2	3	4	5
Nada	Sólo un poco	Algo	Bastante	Mucho

- -

Contrato de Confidencialidad

Entiendo que cualquier cosa que diga o haga dentro del grupo no sera divulgada por los líderes a nadie fuera del grupo, incluyendo a mis padres, amigos y maestros. Entiendo que la única excepción a esto es si revelo información sobre mí o alguna otra persona estando en peligro; entonces, el líder del grupo tendrán que compartir esa información para mantenerme a mí o a la otra persona a salvo.

También entiendo que no puedo hablarle a nadie más sobre lo que los demás miembros dicen o hacen dentro del grupo. Esto incluye hablar con mis padres, hermanos, hermanas y amistades. Entiendo que los otros miembros del grupo confiarán en mí al compartir sus secretos, y que hablar sobre lo que ellos dicen sería traicionar su confianza.

Al firmar este contrato, acepto no hablar con nadie fuera del grupo sobre lo que se dice en el grupo.

_____   _____
Firma del miembro del grupo   **Fecha**

Feelings for Feelings Grab Bag:
Spanish Version

Asustado *(Scared)*	**Orgulloso** *(Proud)*
Tímido *(Shy)*	**Desilusionado** *(Disappointed)*
Valiente *(Brave)*	**Confundido** *(Confused)*
Triste *(Sad)*	**Feliz** *(Happy)*
Sorprendido *(Surprised)*	**Apenado/ Abochornado** *(Embarrassed)*
Frustrado *(Frustrated)*	**Emocionado** *(Excited)*
Relajado *(Relaxed)*	**Tenso/Estresado** *(Stressed)*
Avergonzado *(Ashamed)*	**Confiado** *(Confident)*

APPENDIX D-1c From Waterman and Walker (2000). Copyright 2000 by The Guilford Press.

Secrets for Secret Pooling—Low-Trust Version (Younger Students): Spanish Version

Secreto

Estoy en una pandilla.
(I am in a gang.)

Instrucciones:
1. Leer este secreto en voz alta como si fuera tuyo.
2. Decir cómo te sentirías si fuera tu secreto.

- -

Secreto

He fumado marijuana.
(I have smoked marijuana.)

Instrucciones:
1. Leer este secreto en voz alta como si fuera tuyo.
2. Decir cómo te sentirías si fuera tu secreto.

- -

Secreto

He robado una tienda.
(I have shoplifted.)

Instrucciones:
1. Leer este secreto en voz alta como si fuera tuyo.
2. Decir cómo te sentirías si fuera tu secreto.

- -

Secreto

Yo repetí un grado escolar.
(I have been held back a grade.)

Instrucciones:
1. Leer este secreto en voz alta como si fuera tuyo.
2. Decir cómo te sentirías si fuera tu secreto.

- -

Secreto

He sido detenido por la policía.
(I have been picked up by the police.)

Instrucciones:
1. **Leer este secreto en voz alta como si fuera tuyo.**
2. **Decir cómo te sentirías si fuera tu secreto.**

- -

Secreto

Mis padres se están divorciando.
(My parents are getting a divorce.)

Instrucciones:
1. **Leer este secreto en voz alta como si fuera tuyo.**
2. **Decir cómo te sentirías si fuera tu secreto.**

- -

Secreto

Hago trampa en los exámenes.
(I cheat on tests.)

Instrucciones:
1. **Leer este secreto en voz alta como si fuera tuyo.**
2. **Decir cómo te sentirías si fuera tu secreto.**

- -

Secreto

Mi papá está en la cárcel.
(My dad is in jail.)

Instrucciones:
1. **Leer este secreto en voz alta como si fuera tuyo.**
2 **Decir cómo te sentirías si fuera tu secreto.**

- -

Secreto

He estado borracho.
(I have gotten drunk.)

Instrucciones:
1. **Leer este secreto en voz alta como si fuera tuyo.**
2. **Decir cómo te sentirías si fuera tu secreto.**

- -

Secreto

A veces quisiera matarme.
(I sometimes feel like killing myself.)

Instrucciones:
1. **Leer este secreto en voz alta como si fuera tuyo.**
2. **Decir cómo te sentirías si fuera tu secreto.**

- -

Secreto

_____

Instrucciones:
1. **Leer este secreto en voz alta como si fuera tuyo.**
2. **Decir cómo te sentirías si fuera tu secreto.**

- -

Secreto

_____

Instrucciones:
1. **Leer este secreto en voz alta como si fuera tuyo.**
2. **Decir cómo te sentirías si fuera tu secreto.**

- -

Secreto

_____

Instrucciones:
1. **Leer este secreto en voz alta como si fuera tuyo.**
2. **Decir cómo te sentirías si fuera tu secreto.**

- -

Secreto

_____

Instrucciones:
1. **Leer este secreto en voz alta como si fuera tuyo.**
2. **Decir cómo te sentirías si fuera tu secreto.**

- -

Secrets for Secret Pooling— Low-Trust Version (Older Students): Spanish Version

Secreto

Estoy en una pandilla.
(I am in a gang.)

Instrucciones:
1. **Leer este secreto en voz alta como si fuera tuyo.**
2. **Decir cómo te sentirías si fuera tu secreto.**

- -

Secreto

He fumado marijuana.
(I have smoked marijuana.)

Instrucciones:
1. **Leer este secreto en voz alta como si fuera tuyo.**
2. **Decir cómo te sentirías si fuera tu secreto.**

- -

Secreto

He robado una tienda.
(I have shoplifted.)

Instrucciones:
1. **Leer este secreto en voz alta como si fuera tuyo.**
2. **Decir cómo te sentirías si fuera tu secreto.**

- -

Secreto

Niñas: Estuve embarazada y aborté.
(Girls: I got pregnant and had an abortion.)
O
Niños: Mi novia quedó embarazada de mí y abortó.
(Guys: I got my girlfriend pregnant and she had an abortion.)

Instrucciones:
1. **Leer este secreto en voz alta como si fuera tuyo.**
2. **Decir cómo te sentirías si fuera tu secreto.**

- -

Secreto

He sido arrestado por la policía.
(I have been picked up by the police.)

Instrucciones:
1. **Leer este secreto en voz alta como si fuera tuyo.**
2. **Decir cómo te sentirías si fuera tu secreto.**

- -

Secreto

Mis padres se están divorciando.
(My parents are getting a divorce.)

Instrucciones:
1. **Leer este secreto en voz alta como si fuera tuyo.**
2. **Decir cómo te sentirías si fuera tu secreto.**

- -

Secreto

He tenido sexo.
(I have had sex.)

Instrucciones:
1. **Leer este secreto en voz alta como si fuera tuyo.**
2. **Decir cómo te sentirías si fuera tu secreto.**

- -

Secreto

Mi papá está en la cárcel.
(My dad is in jail.)

Instrucciones:
1. **Leer este secreto en voz alta como si fuera tuyo.**
2. **Decir cómo te sentirías si fuera tu secreto.**

- -

Secreto

He estado borracho.
(I have gotten drunk.)

Instrucciones:
1. **Leer este secreto en voz alta como si fuera tuyo.**
2. **Decir cómo te sentirías si fuera tu secreto.**

Secreto

A veces quisiera matarme.
(I sometimes feel like killing myself.)

Instrucciones:
1. Leer este secreto en voz alta como si fuera tuyo.
2. Decir cómo te sentirías si fuera tu secreto.

- -

Secreto

_____

Instrucciones:
1. Leer este secreto en voz alta como si fuera tuyo.
2. Decir cómo te sentirías si fuera tu secreto.

- -

Secreto

_____

Instrucciones:
1. Leer este secreto en voz alta como si fuera tuyo.
2. Decir cómo te sentirías si fuera tu secreto.

- -

Secreto

_____

Instrucciones:
1. Leer este secreto en voz alta como si fuera tuyo.
2. Decir cómo te sentirías si fuera tu secreto.

- -

Secreto

_____

Instrucciones:
1. Leer este secreto en voz alta como si fuera tuyo.
2. Decir cómo te sentirías si fuera tu secreto.

- -

Respuestas de Ayuda

Maneras de Ayudar a una Persona Que Esta Molesta, Triste, o Tiene un Problema

1. **Escucha cuidadosamente** lo que dice la persona. Míralo/a directamente y ponle mucha atención. No le interrumpas. Trata de entender lo que esta sintiendo.

2. **Comunícale a la persona que comprendes y entiendes sus y sentimientos.** Por ejemplo: "Te debes sentir muy triste por eso," "Eso te puso furioso/a," o "Eso debe de ser tan difícil para ti."

3. **Comparte una experiencia similar para** que la persona no se sienta sola. Mantén el enfoque de la conversación en la persona con el problema, no en ti.

Respuestas Que No Son de Ayuda

1. **Decirle a la persona lo que debe hacer.** No des consejos.

2. **Criticar a la persona con el problema.** Quieres ayudar a que la persona se sienta aceptada, no que se sienta mal por compartir su problema.

3. **Hacer muchas preguntas por curiosidad.** Concéntrate con lo que esta pasando con la persona y no en lo que tú quieres saber.

APPENDIX D-1e From Waterman and Walker (2000). Copyright 2000 by The Guilford Press.

Pasos Para Resolver Problemas

Hot-Head Cool-Head Game Cards: Spanish Version

PROBLEMA	**PROBLEMA**
PROBLEMA	**PROBLEMA**
PROBLEMA	**PROBLEMA**
PROBLEMA	**PROBLEMA**
PROBLEMA	**PROBLEMA**
PROBLEMA	**PROBLEMA**
PROBLEMA	**PROBLEMA**
PROBLEMA	**PROBLEMA**

Mi hermano/a me estaba molestando.	**Mis padres me castigaron sin razón.**
Otro chico estaba molestando a mi amigo/a.	**Otro chico tomo algo que era mio.**
Mi novio/a salio con otra persona.	**Alguien hizo trampa para salir mejor que yo.**
Otro chico dijo algo acerca de mi madre.	**Mi maestra la tenía conmigo.**
Alguien me hizo un comentario racista.	**Otro chico me empujo.**
Otro chico robo mi dinero.	**Me culparon por algo que no hize.**
Mi amigo le contó a alguien un secreto mío.	**Otro niño me insultó.**
Mi mejor amigo/a salió con mi novio/a.	**Mi hermano me quitó mi dinero.**

ALTERNATIVA	ALTERNATIVA
ALTERNATIVA	ALTERNATIVA
ALTERNATIVA	ALTERNATIVA
ALTERNATIVA	ALTERNATIVA
ALTERNATIVA	ALTERNATIVA
ALTERNATIVA	ALTERNATIVA
ALTERNATIVA	ALTERNATIVA
ALTERNATIVA	ALTERNATIVA

✳✳**CALIENTE**✳✳	✳✳**CALIENTE**✳✳
✳✳**CALIENTE**✳✳	✳✳**CALIENTE**✳✳
✳✳**CALIENTE**✳✳	✳✳**CALIENTE**✳✳
✳✳**CALIENTE**✳✳	✳✳**CALIENTE**✳✳
❄❄❄**FRÍO**❄❄❄	❄❄❄**FRÍO**❄❄❄
❄❄❄**FRÍO**❄❄❄	❄❄❄**FRÍO**❄❄❄
❄❄❄**FRÍO**❄❄❄	❄❄❄**FRÍO**❄❄❄
❄❄❄**FRÍO**❄❄❄	❄❄❄**FRÍO**❄❄❄

CONSECUENCIA	**CONSECUENCIA**
CONSECUENCIA	**CONSECUENCIA**
CONSECUENCIA	**CONSECUENCIA**
CONSECUENCIA	**CONSECUENCIA**
CONSECUENCIA	**CONSECUENCIA**
CONSECUENCIA	**CONSECUENCIA**
CONSECUENCIA	**CONSECUENCIA**
CONSECUENCIA	**CONSECUENCIA**

Consecuencia a largo plazo para ti	Consecuencia a corto plazo para ti
Consecuencia a largo plazo para ti	Consecuencia a corto plazo para ti
Consecuencia a largo plazo para ti	Consecuencia a corto plazo para ti
Consecuencia a largo plazo para ti	Consecuencia a corto plazo para ti
Consecuencia a largo plazo para ellos	Consecuencia a corto plazo para ellos
Consecuencia a largo plazo para ellos	Consecuencia a corto plazo para ellos
Consecuencia a largo plazo para ellos	Consecuencia a corto plazo para ellos
Consecuencia a largo plazo para ellos	Consecuencia a corto plazo para ellos

Respuestas Cool-Head

Durante la siguiente semana, observa dos situaciones en que te enojas.

Usa respuestas "cool-head" en estas situaciones. Anota estas situaciones aquí debajo o ven preparado para hablar de ellas la pro xima semana.

Si usaste una respuesta "hot-head," anotala aquí y también escribe una posible respuesta "cool-head."

Yo me enoje cuando:

_____

_____

La respuesta "cool-head" que usé fue:

_____

_____

Yo me enoje cuando:

_____

_____

La respuesta "cool-head" que usé fue:

_____

_____

Yo usé una respuesta "hot-head" cuando:

_____

_____

La respuesta "cool-head" que pude haber usado fue:

_____

_____

Nombre: _____

Labels for Labeling Game: Spanish Version

BUEN ESTUDIANTE (Good student)	**MANDÓN** (Bossy)
FLOJO (Lazy)	**MASCOTA DE LA MAESTRA** (Teacher's pet)
AMISTOSO (Friendly)	**BUEN ATLETA** (Good athlete)
TÍMIDO (Shy)	**PRESUMIDO** (Snobby)
SEXY	**AYUDANTE** (Helpful)
ENOJADO (Angry)	**SOLITARIO** (Loner)
CASANOVA (Player)	**CHISMOSO** (Big mouth)

APPENDIX D-3 From Waterman and Walker (2000). Copyright 2000 by The Guilford Press.

Escala de Educación y Carrera Profesional

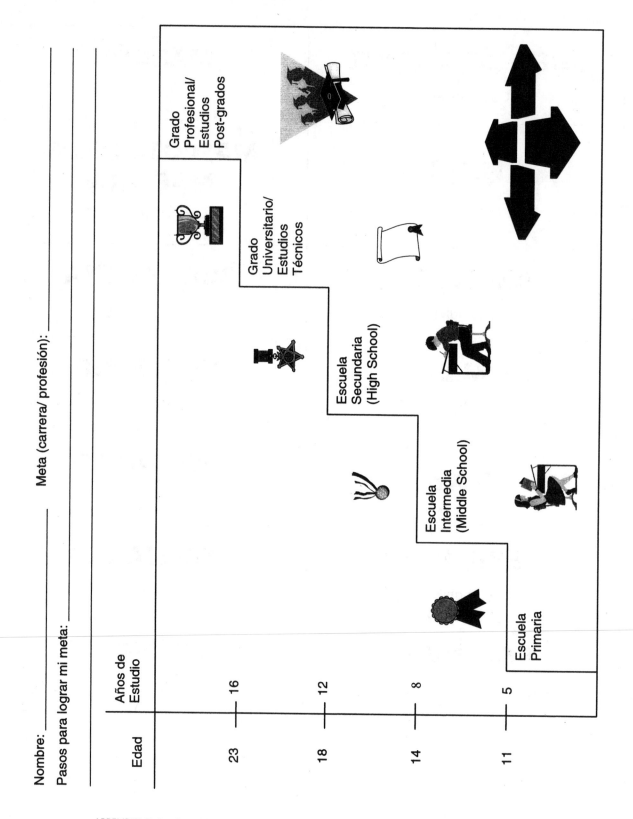

Nombre: _____

Meta (carrera/ profesión): _____

Pasos para lograr mi meta: _____

Edad	Años de Estudio	
23	16	Grado Profesional/ Estudios Post-grados
18	12	Grado Universitario/ Estudios Técnicos
14	8	Escuela Secundaria (High School)
11	5	Escuela Intermedia (Middle School)
		Escuela Primaria

APPENDIX D-4a   From Waterman and Walker (2000). Copyright 2000 by The Guilford Press.

Mis Metas

Declaro metas para mí y trabajo para cumplir con ellas.

Mis metas para este año escolar son:

1. _____

_____

2. _____

_____

3. _____

_____

Para lograr esas metas voy a:

1. _____

_____

2. _____

_____

3. _____

_____

_____   _____
Firma   **Fecha**

Resistiendo la Presión Entre Compañeros

Situación en la cual fuí presionado/a:

_____

_____

_____

Resistí!!!!!!
Estrategias que usé:

_____

_____

_____

_____

_____

Me dí por vencido/a . . .
La razón fue:

_____

_____

_____

_____

_____

Situación en la cual fuí presionado/a:

_____

_____

_____

Resistí!!!!!
Estrategias que usé:

_____

_____

_____

_____

_____

Me dí por vencido/a . . .
La razón fue:

_____

_____

_____

_____

_____

Nombre: _____

Reacciones al Stress Post-traumático

- Ocurren luego de un evento que nos da mucho miedo.

- Son muy comunes entre estudiantes que han sido expuestos a violencia en el hogar, la escuela o la vecindad.

- Pueden ocurrir si eres la víctima de violencia o si vez un acto de violencia.

- Son reacciones *normales* a situaciones fuera de lo común.

- Hay tres tipos de reacciones.

1. *Reexperimentar el trauma.*

   a. Recuerdos o pensamientos acerca del trauma se aparecen de repente en tu mente.

   b. Soñar con lo que pasó una y otra vez.

   c. Sentir que el evento traumático esta pasando otra vez, como "flashbacks".

   d. Ponerte muy nervioso o incómodo si te acercas al lugar donde ocurrió.

2. *Evitando el trauma.*

   a. Evitar personas, lugares o actividades que te hacen recordar el trauma.

   b. Sentirte alejado de otras personas, como si no sintieras nada.

   c. Tener menos interés en cosas que te gustaban antes del trauma.

   d. Pensar que no vas a tener una profesión o familia o que vas a morir siendo jóven.

3. *Sentirse mas agitado.*

   a. Tener problemas al dormir o mantenerte dormido.

   b. Sentirte irritable o enojarte muy facilmente.

   c. Estar distraído o tener dificultad prestando atención.

   d. Estar super-alerta en lugares donde pueda haber peligro, o sobresaltarse con mucha facilidad.

APPENDIX D-6a From Waterman and Walker (2000). Copyright 2000 by The Guilford Press.

Disks for Posttraumatic Stress Reactions: Spanish Version

Reexperimentar	Reexperimentar	Reexperimentar
Reexperimentar	Reexperimentar	Reexperimentar
Reexperimentar	Reexperimentar	Reexperimentar
Reexperimentar	Reexperimentar	Reexperimentar
Reexperimentar	Reexperimentar	Reexperimentar

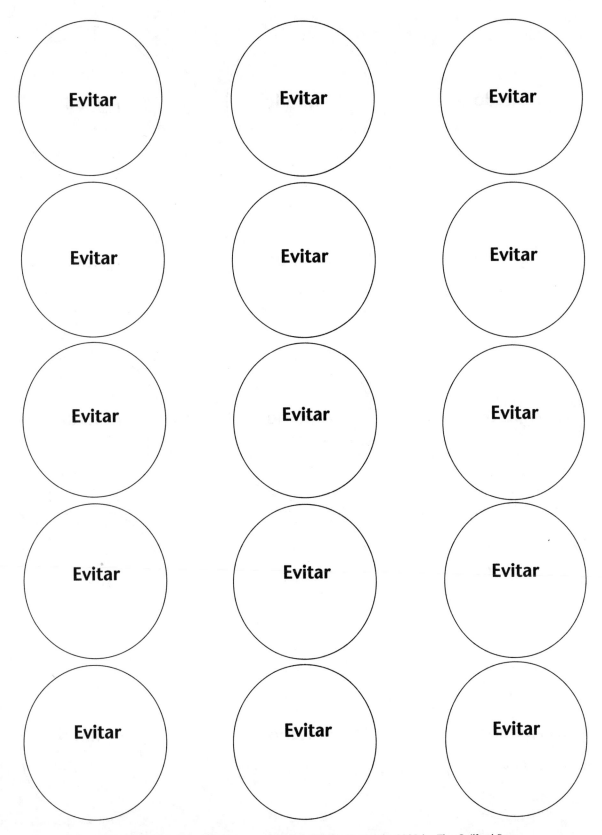

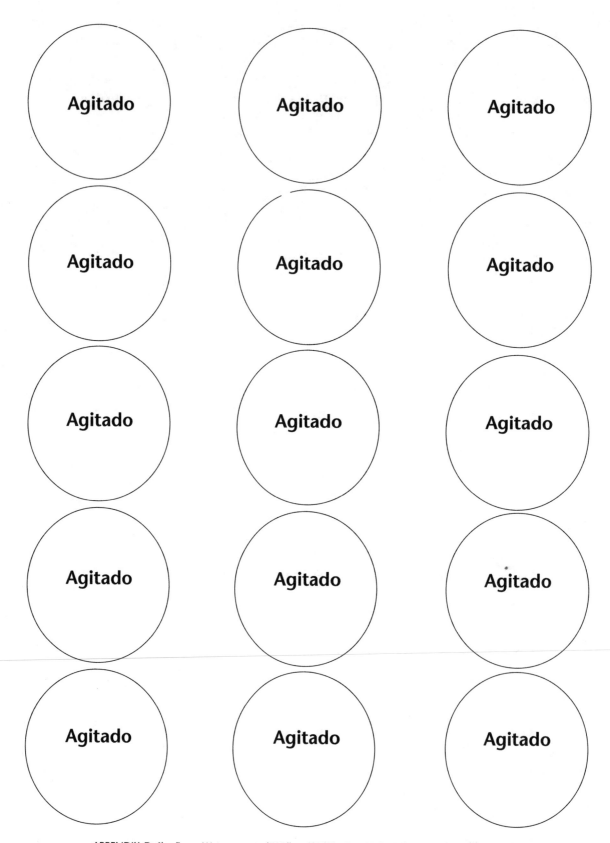

Lo Que Nos Gusta de Ti

Nombre: _____

Miembro del grupo   **Lo que me gusta de ti es . . .**

_____   _____

                                  _____

_____   _____

                                  _____

_____   _____

                                  _____

_____   _____

                                  _____

_____   _____

                                  _____

_____   _____

                                  _____

_____   _____

                                  _____

_____   _____

                                  _____

Certificado de Reconocimiento

Este certificado se le otorga a

_____

por haber completado con éxito el Programa SPARK

este _____ de _____, _____.

_____
Líder del Grupo

_____
Líder del Grupo

APPENDIX D-7b   From Waterman and Walker (2000). Copyright 2000 by The Guilford Press.

References

Armsden, G. C., & Greenberg, M. T. (1987). The Inventory of Parent and Peer Attachment: Individual differences and their relationship to psychological well-being in adolescence. *Journal of Youth and Adolescence, 16*, 427–453.

Briere, J. (1996). *Trauma Symptom Checklist for Children (TSCC) professional manual.* Odessa, FL: Psychological Assessment Resources.

Campbell, C. A. (1991). Group guidance for academically undermotivated children. *Elementary School Guidance and Counseling, 25*, 302–307.

Goodman, G., & Esterly, G. (1988). *The talk book: The intimate science of communicating in close relationships.* Emmaus, PA: Rodale Press.

Kazdin, A. E. (1993). Adolescent mental health: Prevention and treatment programs. *American Psychologist, 48*, 127–141.

Pedro-Carroll, J. L. (1985). *The Children of Divorce Intervention Program procedures manual.* Rochester, NY: University of Rochester Center for Community Study.

Phinney, J. S. (1992). The Multigroup Ethnic Identity Measure: A new scale for use with diverse groups. *Journal of Adolescent Research, 7*, 156–176.

Richters, J. E., & Saltzman, W. (1990). *Survey of children's exposure to community violence: Parent report.* Washington, DC: National Institute of Mental Health.

Rosenberg, M. (1979). *Conceiving the self.* New York: Basic Books.

Slaby, R. G., & Wilson-Brewer, R. (1992). *Vignettes developed for the evaluation of violence prevention curricula targeting middle school students.* Newton, MA: Education Development Center.

Swearingen, E.M., & Cohen, L. H. (1985). Measurement of adolescents' life events: The Junior High Life Experiences Survey. *American Journal of Community Psychology, 13*, 69–85.

Watt, D. (1998). *I'm in charge here: Exposure to community violence, perceptions of control, and academic and aggressive outcome in inner-city youth.* Unpublished doctoral dissertation, University of California, Los Angeles.

Index